# ChatGPT Made Simple

How Anyone Can Harness AI To Streamline
Their Work, Study & Everyday Tasks To Boost
Productivity & Maintain Competitive Edge By
Mastering Prompt Engineering

## D. Nardo Publications

# Contents

# A GIFT FOR YOU

To get the most out of this book, there's a special, FREE prompts guide tailored just for you. This isn't just another freebie—it's your golden key to a more efficient, innovative, and tech-savvy future.

## What's Inside:

- Seven Industry Breakdowns: From everyday life to engineering, discover how to unlock the full potential of ChatGPT across various fields.

- Comprehensive Roadmap: Tips, role-based prompts, and experimental 'fill in the blank' prompts for high-quality ChatGPT interactions.

- Exclusive Bonus: The 52 BEST All-Purpose ChatGPT Prompts to skyrocket productivity, no matter your industry.

## How to Get It:

Simply go to brechtdinardo.com/freeguide or scan the QR code below!

# Introduction

I f you are anything like me, the first thing that comes to your mind when you hear the words "artificial intelligence" (AI) isn't being able to do work that would have taken you hours upon hours in the span of 5 minutes.

It isn't overcoming writer's block, which can be infinitely infuriating. It certainly isn't doing away with the more, shall we say, frustrating bits of customer service work with the miracle known as chatbots. No, what probably comes to your mind is the doomsday scenarios that Hollywood movies have been training into us for years, if not decades. This is a shame because these scenarios couldn't be farther from the truth, especially considering how we are already living in an age where AI is practically a part of every facet of our lives. It has been for a while now, though the effects have been more noticeable in recent years.

This wondrous age that saves us time, energy, and effort, all while increasing our productivity and creativity, is the ChatGPT age. ChatGPT is a revolutionary language model created by OpenAI. Since its inception, it has made its presence known in practically every industry. In the process, it has begun to utterly transform these industries and redefine the very words "possible," "creative," and "productive."

Don't believe me? Take a look at high school and college students these days. These younger generations, being the early adopters that they so often are, often use ChatGPT when writing college-level essays. That certainly beats staring at a blank page for hours and then giving up to pay someone to write your essay. They have also used ChatGPT to finish their homework and assignments. If you think these students must be in the minority, think again. Current statistics show that 89% of all students use ChatGPT to get homework help (Kochovski, 2023).

We often think of younger generations as those we have to guide and teach things to. In this case, however, they have something to teach us because just as ChatGPT can help students do better academically, it can help you do much better at your job without too much effort. Not only that, but it can increase your productivity and creativity, reduce your stress and anxiety levels, and improve the quality of your work. Most importantly, it can help you stay current in a rapidly evolving job market, because here's the thing: AI isn't going anywhere. It is here to stay, and its impact on the job market is already very tangible. If you mean to stay in said job market, then you have to get acquainted with ChatGPT, figure out its ins and outs, and keep up with new trends.

Given how new and unfamiliar ChatGPT is to you, you may be hesitant to do this. Luckily, this is where ChatGPT Made Simple comes in. In this book, you will learn how to use ChatGPT well and efficiently. More specifically, you'll learn how to craft the perfect questions or instructions (we call these 'prompts') that will guide ChatGPT to give you the exact response or result you're looking for.

You will get to see just how ChatGPT can be integrated into your professional and personal life, thereby increasing your potential by leaps and bounds. Last but not least, you'll discover how you can use ChatGPT to create a better work-life balance for yourself and reduce the stress and anxiety you experience daily.

Put simply, by diving into ChatGPT Made Simple, you will improve your life in many different ways and become a part of an ongoing revolution pioneers such as Bill Gates are already a part of, going off of how the tech genius is known to praise ChatGPT's ability to do anything and everything, from giving medical advice to people with limited resources to teaching math in an easy and very understandable manner (Mok, 2023).

With that in mind, how exactly can you use ChatGPT to suit your own needs and make your life easier? How can you use it to do the best work possible while saving yourself a great deal of time and energy? Let's find out!

# Chapter One

# ChatGPT Revealed: The Power Behind Human-like Text Generation

*"By 2025, the global AI market is projected to reach $190 billion, growing at 40.2% from 2020 to 2025."*

Shanal Govender

First things first: What precisely is ChatGPT, and how does it work? What are its capabilities and features, and what exactly can you do with it? The short answer to that question is "many, many things." Imagine having a friend who knows all the answers to your questions. It's like a super-smart helper on your computer or phone that can chat with you about anything you want. As for the long answer...

ChatGPT uses the magic of machine learning algorithms to understand and generate text that is as human-like as possible (UCO: ChatGPT and AI Technology, n.d.). Machine learning algorithms work much like a chef trying new recipes. Every attempt provides new insights and fine-tunes the chef's skill. To generate and refine its skills, ChatGPT has been trained using a plethora of data, including actual books, numerous websites, and stacks of articles. Thus, it has developed a library of information and knowledge that it can turn to for practically any matter. Naturally, Chat-GPT cannot provide information on every little topic known to man.

However, its pool of knowledge is still incredibly vast, enabling it to be helpful to us mere humans in an array of industries, such as:

# Customer Service

An industry where ChatGPT undoubtedly comes very handy in, as you'll see in greater detail in coming chapters. Customer service can be… challenging, to put it really mildly, because you often have to deal with the same kinds of questions and because the customers you end up having to deal with aren't always nice. ChatGPT can help in both of these circumstances by automating incoming queries (Dreamanart Team, 2023). That way, you and the company you work for save time, you end up not having to copy-paste the same answer to the same query 50 million times, and you get to the more urgent queries more quickly. In other words, ChatGPT makes your job easier and makes you better at it.

Moreover, ChatGPT lends a personalized touch to every message it sends, adding a 'human' feel to its interactions and fostering brand loyalty. Imagine having a helping hand available 24/7, answering queries and building better relationships with your customers. What's more, ChatGPT continually learns from past interactions, as we discussed, much like a good customer service rep remembering frequent customers and their preferences. By storing and analyzing previous queries, it keeps honing its skills, becoming an ever more effective tool for your customer service needs.

Now, the usefulness of ChatGPT reaches far beyond the customer service realm, of course. Though we'll be digging deeper into this in the coming chapters, here's a sneak peek at how you can harness this tool across many industries. Bear in mind this is just the tip of the iceberg when it comes to the myriad possibilities that ChatGPT brings to any scenario:

a detailed, on-topic answer. That's what prompt engineering does: it's about asking the right question in the right way to get the best response.

Understanding this, it becomes clear that the key to optimizing Chat-GPT's performance lies not only in asking the right questions but also in continually enriching its knowledge base. The good thing is that your prompts feed ChatGPT tons of data. Thanks to all this data, it can understand your thoughts and feelings and, in a sense, empathize with you (Tran Nguyen, 2023). Being able to empathize with other people is a vital part of everyday communication, which some of us struggle with. Humans typically develop this capacity when they are children, but they can also keep doing so as adults. ChatGPT develops it with every bit of information it trains itself with. It implements the "Theory of Mind" to understand what people mean, not just what they say. It's like it puts itself in our shoes.

What makes ChatGPT even more impressive is its understanding of languages. Yes, it can understand and respond in many different languages, which makes it incredibly powerful, not to mention useful. It is these abilities and the way ChatGPT can keep learning and improving upon itself over time that allow it to serve a multitude of purposes.

Furthermore, you can improve the quality and authenticity of those responses as time passes. You can even use ChatGPT as an alternative to a Google search. Whether you can effectively do this or not will depend on how much data it has learned from and your knack for asking the right questions.

I have created a free resource to help you with this task, so please take a moment to check out the 'ChatGPT Prompts Cheat Sheet'. It isn't just a simple guide; it's a vital tool I've crafted to help you construct those pitch-perfect questions that can unlock the full potential of ChatGPT.

I've personally found it to be an invaluable asset, and I'm confident you will too. To access it, simply go to brechtdinardo.com/freeguide or scan the QR code below:

**Note:** If you can't find it in your inbox after claiming it, there's a chance your spam folder might have sneakily claimed it as a treasure, so make sure to check there too!

## What Are Its Limitations?

While ChatGPT is a fantastic tool, it has its limitations. These limitations partly stem from ChatGPT being a program, not a human being. As such, it lacks certain basic things that any human being would have, such as common sense and emotional intelligence (Marr, 2023). Of course, it can mimic these if it has been trained on enough data (as I just mentioned) but only to a certain degree, and even then, some of the responses it creates might sound inauthentic. Time will only tell if AI will get better at such things.

Another significant limitation, which veers more to the technical side, is generating long-form, well-structured content. Typically, ChatGPT does better with shorter texts. On top of that, it has trouble multitasking. That is not to say it cannot multitask, but simply that it finds it to be a challenge. In all honesty, this is something that human beings struggle with as well, so it is not that hard to believe ChatGPT would too.

Then there's the fact that ChatGPT can have limited knowledge, as vast as its library might be, like I mentioned before. That might sound like an oxymoron, but it makes sense when you think about it. After all, ChatGPT can only know as much as it is "taught." If you don't give ChatGPT new data, then it won't learn new things and the content it will generate will be confined to what it already knows. Similarly, the kind of knowledge you feed ChatGPT can cause it to become biased. Using the word "biased" in relation to AI sounds bizarre, but think about it: If the content you are feeding ChatGPT only ever features '60s stereotypes of women, then wouldn't any and all of the content it generates about women automatically become biased?

That said, it's worth noting that ChatGPT is a continually evolving tool. From its earliest inception, each subsequent version has been a significant improvement on the previous one. Now we've reached the stage of ChatGPT-4, a sophisticated model that addresses many of the limitations found in GPT-3. This ongoing evolution assures us that future iterations will keep refining the technology, addressing existing challenges even more effectively.

# Key Takeaways:

- ChatGPT is an AI chatbot that generates human-like text using machine learning, revolutionizing many industries.

- It's widely useful in fields like business, customer service, marketing, content creation, education, and many more.

- 'Prompt engineering' is the art of crafting effective questions, statements, or instructions to interact with ChatGPT intelligently and accurately.

- Mastery of 'prompt engineering' optimizes your results when using ChatGPT.

- This book includes an invaluable 'ChatGPT Prompts Cheat Sheet' to supercharge your prompt creation and unlock ChatGPT's full potential.

- Despite its strengths, ChatGPT has limitations in long-form content and multitasking.

- While ChatGPT may face challenges with long-form content and multitasking, it's amazingly versatile and is consistently evolving for superior performance.

# Test Your Knowledge:

**1. Which sectors can benefit significantly from using the ChatGPT AI chatbot?**

a) Retail and e-commerce only

b) Business, customer service, marketing, content creation, education, and many more

c) Limited to tech industries

**2. What is the term for the skill of formulating effective interactions with ChatGPT?**

a) Prompt development

b) Command generation

c) Prompt engineering

**3. Despite its versatility, does ChatGPT have certain limitations?**

a) No, it is capable of any task as long as you have a powerful prompt

b) Yes, it sometimes struggles with tasks unrelated to text generation

c) Yes, it can struggle with long-form content and multitasking

**Answers: 1-b, 2-c, 3-c**

Now that you've got the hang of what ChatGPT is all about, it's time to roll up your sleeves and dive right in! In the next chapter, we'll navigate the practical aspects—setting up your account and getting to know the system. Let's get to it!

## Chapter Two

# Kickstarting Your ChatGPT Adventure

*"To me, artificial intelligence like ChatGPT, used by those with wisdom, knowledge, and experience, can authentically enhance the distribution of intelligence and information in a positive way. Though when used by deceptive, inexperienced, and greedy fools...it can be a dangerous tool."*

Loren Weisman

It's time to kickstart your very own ChatGPT adventure. Indeed, you need to know how to use ChatGPT to enjoy its benefits and features. This process begins with setting up your account. That done, you'll need to familiarize yourself with ChatGPT's interface, learn the basic terms and concepts—like text tokens, for example—you'll encounter here, and understand the different model versions you might be dealing with.

## Setting Up Your Account

If you are anything like me, the idea of setting up another account on top of the 100 different accounts for 100 different things you already have sounds annoying. How are you supposed to remember all those different passwords, anyways? But trust me, creating *this* account will be well worth it, and it's pretty simple too.

## Step #1: Sign Up

Head to **OpenAI.com** and click **"Sign Up"** to set up your account. Use an email address (a spare Gmail account can help keep things tidy), and pick a strong, memorable password.

## Create your account

Please note that phone verification is required for signup. Your number will only be used to verify your identity for security purposes.

Email address

Continue

Already have an account?  Log in

OR

G    Continue with Google

▦    Continue with Microsoft Account

**Note:** ChatGPT is currently unavailable in Russia, Ukraine, China, Iran, and Egypt (Miley, 2023). You can access the ChatGPT page using a VPN if you are in these regions.

## Step #2: Verify Your Info

Check your inbox for a verification email and click **"Verify Email Address."**

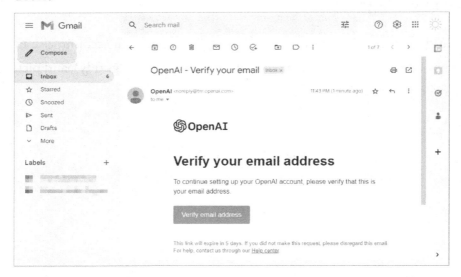

Next, you'll be redirected to a page saying "Tell Us About You" — no need to spill your life story, save that for dating apps. Just enter your name and click **"Continue."**

Now, you will need to verify your phone number. Enter it, and you'll receive a six-digit code. Key in the code, and there you have it, your account is set up!

## Step #3: Log In

Now, head back to the ChatGPT **"Login"** page. Enter your email address and password to access your ChatGPT account. Enjoy exploring!

# Getting To Know the Interface

Now on to the big question: How do you use ChatGPT after creating your account? When you log into your OpenAI account and select the ChatGPT interface, you'll land on a page that lays out all the amazing things ChatGPT can do and its limitations. It's like a quick guide to the possibilities with ChatGPT.

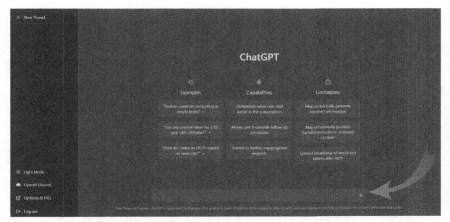

At the end of this page, there's a dedicated space for you to type your messages, a.k.a' prompts' (queries, instructions, or any issues you're facing).

When you enter a query or prompt, ChatGPT swings into action. It thoroughly analyzes your input to understand it to the core. Then, it translates it into its own language (binary), extracting all necessary data to serve you best. Its response will be "Sent in Chat" to you.

The great thing about ChatGPT, as I mentioned earlier, is that the more you use it, the more data it will collect. The more data it collects, the better and more refined its future responses will be. Giving feedback is helpful if you want to further help it refine its responses. You can do this by typing something like "Resend your answer. Explain this to me in a shorter, more concise way" or by giving it a thumbs-up or thumbs-down.

If, after this, you still don't like the response you're getting (or if there was a technical glitch requiring you to get a new one), you can click on the "regenerate response" button.

Something that I love and find extremely helpful in ChatGPT is that you can always start a new conversation by clicking on the "New Chat" / "New Thread" button, which you can find on the left-hand side of the screen. You can then have a separate "Conversation" for each of your topics. That way, ChatGPT will remember whatever you discussed in earlier conversations. Thus, ChatGPT can respond to what you say within the given context.

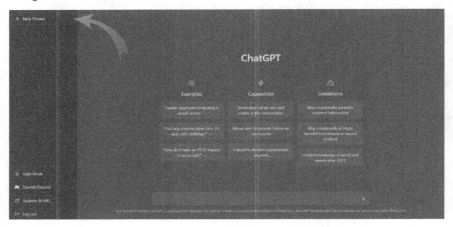

Now, since you most likely don't have the same kind of memory that ChatGPT does—assuming you are not superhuman, of course—ChatGPT keeps a history of your previous conversations. You can scroll through this chat history to refresh your memory at any time. If you do have a superhuman memory, you can turn off this chat history as well.

## ChatGPT Mobile App

If you're often on the move, you might find the ChatGPT mobile app useful. It's a straightforward way to handle emails, draft quick notes, or ask questions when you're away from your computer. Just go to your app store and search for "ChatGPT." Make sure OpenAI is listed as the developer to ensure you're getting the real deal. It's a handy tool to have in your pocket.

# Understanding Model Versions

As you know by now, there are different versions of ChatGPT, such as GPT-3.5 and GPT-4. GPT-4 isn't just newer; it's a powerhouse. Let's check out the features that set it apart:

## Multimodal Advantage

Unlike GPT-3.5, GPT-4 can accept multiple input types, such as text and images. This flexibility is a game-changer, especially for individuals working with visuals and text - think graphic designers, content creators, and digital marketers.

## A Leap in Reasoning

If GPT-3.5 was a budding scholar, consider GPT-4 the seasoned academic. It is so much better at this, in fact, that it can pass standardized tests, otherwise known as the bane of your existence when you were in high school. This doesn't extend to just high school tests, though. ChatGPT-4 is known to have nailed the bar exam and other similar advanced tests, something previous versions couldn't do. Thanks to these reasoning capabilities, GPT-4 can rank among the top 10% of students taking the bar—if it were an actual student. Imagine the depth and complexity of the responses you can expect from it.

## Enhanced Intuitiveness

This means it better understands complex queries and delivers more accurate responses. In layman's terms, you'll spend less time refining queries to get the right response.

Note: As of this writing, unlocking GPT-4 requires a monthly membership of $20. I know, I know. But think about it; you only need to swap a couple of your fancy lattes for a ticket to productivity and creativity heaven. It's worth it!

# Key Takeaways

- Setting up a ChatGPT account involves signing up, verifying your email and phone number, and logging in.

- The ChatGPT interface provides a dedicated space for typing prompts, generating responses, and giving feedback.

- The more you use ChatGPT, the more it learns and improves its responses.

- You can initiate new conversations or threads in ChatGPT for different topics.

- GPT-4, a version of ChatGPT, accepts multiple input types and is superior in reasoning.

- GPT -4's enhanced intuitiveness helps understand more complex queries and provide better, more accurate responses.

# Test Your Knowledge

Let's see how well you remember what you have learned with a couple of role-playing exercises, shall we?

**1. You've decided to sign up for ChatGPT. Which website do you need to go to do so?**

a) www.ChatGPT.com

b) www.OpenAI.com

c) www.ChatGPT4.com


**2. Imagine you're using ChatGPT-4, and you want it to explain something to you in a more simplified way. What is one way you can achieve this?**

a) Press the "Reboot" button to restart the system and get a better response

b) Ask ChatGPT-4 something like "Reiterate your answer. Make it simpler for me"

c) Use a coding command to request a simpler response


**3. What are two improvements found in ChatGPT-4 compared to its predecessors?**

a) ChatGPT-4 has enhanced memory capacity and can store vast amounts of information

b) ChatGPT-4 can perform real-time language translation for multiple languages

c) ChatGPT-4 is multimodal, can accept text and image inputs, and has improved reasoning capabilities


Answers: 1-b, 2-b, 3-c

Now that you've got a solid handle on the ChatGPT basics, let's level up! In the next chapter, we're diving into prompts, which will take your productivity and communication skills to a whole new level.

# Chapter Three

# A Prompt Whisperer's Guide To ChatGPT Mastery

*"Artificial Intelligence, deep learning, machine learning —*
*whatever you're doing if you don't understand it — learn it.*
*Because otherwise you're going to be a dinosaur within 3 years."*

Mark Cuban

P rompt engineering is as much a work of art as it is a kind of science. That is to be expected, really, and they are a vital part of using Chat-GPT - as you no doubt have gathered by now. It is how you harness GPT's power to accomplish innumerable tasks. So, with that in mind, let's delve into the essential tips to master this craft.

## The 3 Golden Rules For Effective Prompts

### 1. Provide Context

Whatever prompt you write must have a clear and defined context. Say that you're talking to ChatGPT about strength training and want to know its benefits for your heart. If you write down the prompt:

*"What are the benefits of strength training?"*

You will end up with a hefty list. You will then have to sift through that list to find the heart benefits you're looking for. You can avoid this situation and get the exact answer you want by simply typing:

*"What are the cardiovascular benefits of regular strength training?"*

The words "cardiovascular benefits" in that sentence will provide AI with the context in which you want it to consider your question.

## 2. Be Specific

Specifying your desired format will help you get what you need much faster. Think of it like this: If you were at a restaurant ordering steak, you'd specify whether you wanted it medium-rare or medium-well, right? Being specific in your prompts is no different than being specific in your food orders.

Once again, take the prompt, *"What are the cardiovascular benefits of regular strength training?"* Now, think about how you would like this question answered. Do you want ChatGPT to list all the cardiovascular benefits that come with strength training one by one, or do you want it to deliver the answer in another format? Be specific - and be sure to tell that to ChatGPT.

For instance:

*"Could you please provide <u>a bulleted list</u> of cardiovascular benefits of regular strength training?"*

## 3. Iterate It:

Getting the perfect response on your first try is like hitting a bullseye in your first-ever game of darts - it might happen, but usually, it takes a bit of practice. The old saying, *"If at first you don't succeed, try, try again"* applies perfectly to prompt engineering.

What's really exciting is that ChatGPT uses something called *reinforcement learning from human feedback* (RFHL), which means it will learn from the feedback you provide and adjust its future responses accordingly. Therefore, play around and keep changing your prompts to make them even more contextual and specific. You'd be surprised at how much room for improvement you'll find.

So, ready to put what we've learned into practice? Fire up ChatGPT and try these two prompts:

1. *Discuss the benefits of exercise.*

2. *Write a comprehensive essay highlighting the physical and mental health benefits of regular exercise, supported by scientific studies and personal anecdotes.*

You'll notice that the second prompt yields a more useful response, as it's more specific and carefully tailored to our needs. This underlines the crucial importance of our three golden rules: Context, specificity, and iteration.

Now that you're better acquainted with the basics of prompt engineering, let's move on to more advanced strategies.

# Advanced Strategies

## 1. Adjust Maximum Text Length

One thing you'll notice when playing around with your prompts is that the text may occasionally get cut off, which can be frustrating, to say the least. You can overcome this by adjusting the maximum text length setting using the OpenAI Playground. This way, you can make sure that ChatGPT will be able to give you the complete response you need.

If you think this strategy sounds almost too easy and simple for an 'advanced technique,' then you're right. It is pretty simple and easy, but that's because most strategies for prompt engineering are much less complicated than you'd think.

For an in-depth understanding of the 'Playground,' check out the bonus section on page 119. However, if you prefer a straightforward solution, you can type *"continue with your answer"* whenever you encounter the text cutting off (hat has worked for me).

## 2. Break Down Your Queries

You know by now that a lack of specificity ends up in ChatGPT giving much lengthier (and even rather vague) answers to your queries than you'd like, making it difficult to find the response you need. You can avoid this by breaking down your query into smaller bits.

If you want to inquire about the various benefits of strength training, for instance, you can break down the vague prompt *"What are the benefits of strength training?"* to:

*What are the cardiovascular benefits of strength training?*

*What benefits does strength training have for the musculoskeletal system?*

*What neurological benefits does strength training offer?*

This way, you'll quickly learn the exact benefits you were hoping to find out about. You can break down your queries at the very start of the process and part way through to narrow down the initial response it gives you. This way, you'll even be able to turn your interaction with ChatGPT into an actual conversation, if an educational one, which could be rather fun.

## 3. Decide On A Role

Odds are, you want ChatGPT to provide you with your response in a certain manner. If that's the case, you can assign it a role to adopt and answer the way that a person in that role would.

For example, suppose you're looking for more scientific responses to your questions about strength training. In that case, you can begin your prompt with:

*"You are a cardiologist..."* or

*"You are a neurologist..."* or something of the sort.

If you'd like a more casual, friendly response, you can start your prompt with something like:

*"You are a very close friend..."*

If you're confused as to what a prompt that follows all these rules and guidelines might look like, here is a most basic example:

*Headline: The Physical and Mental Health Benefits of Strength Training.*

*You are a cardiovascular surgeon; please come up with 15 head-lines based on the above headline following the below parameters:*

*Shorter than 100 characters but longer than 60 characters*

*Based on scientifically proven data*

*Using actionable words and sentences*

*Addressing the reader directly*

*Using a tone of voice that is both friendly and professional, as though written by an expert*

*Using a language that is devoid of hard-to-understand terminology*

Again, if you're uncertain whether the prompt you've created is effective (or as effective as you need it to be), ask yourself if you are giving clear directions. Keep your needs and wants in mind as you read over the instructions you've given. Is there anything missing? Do you need to add anything to ensure a need you haven't yet mentioned is met? Remember: Context, specificity and iteration are key.

## Additional Tips & Best Practices

### Identify Your Target Audience

What kind of response you're looking to get to your prompts depends partly on the audience you're trying to reach. Say that you're using Chat-GPT for content creation. Not all content is the same. A post on your blog is vastly different in tone of voice and style of writing than a research paper and an op-ed published in the New York Times. This is only natural because all three of these things target different audiences, so to get the right tone of voice and style in ChatGPT's response, you must identify your audience first and be specific about it (Pietschmann, 2023). Therefore, before writing your prompt, consider who you're trying to reach. You can also ask ChatGPT to give you a hand with this. For instance:

> *"I want to write 3 new posts on my personal blog, which is all about hiking adventures and nature photography. I want to appeal to outdoor enthusiasts and aspiring photographers, but I also want to inspire people interested in starting their own outdoor adventures. Can you help me understand this target audience's demographics, characteristics, interests, and potential questions?"*

Based on this prompt, ChatGPT could then generate a response that might help you to better understand and tailor your content to your specific audience.

## Align Topics With Audience Interests

Once your target audience is defined, ensure that your chosen topic aligns with your target audience's needs, wants, and interests. Let's use another example; suppose your target audience is 20-year-old women in the beauty industry. In that case, odds are they won't be particularly interested in reading about how your gut microbiome affects the progression of Alzheimer's disease. Some of them might be interested in this topic on an individual level, but as a demographic group, this wouldn't be the right subject matter for them.

## Use Relevant Keywords & Themes

Another thing you have to do once you've identified your target demographic is to try and use relevant keywords and themes in your prompt.

This is important because using such things will help you generate more relevant content. Naturally, using the right keywords and themes for your demographic will mean doing a little research. This research will typically take you to Google, where you can review content targeting your demographic and use them to identify relevant keywords.

Let's continue with the example of 20-year-old women interested in the beauty industry. Based on your understanding of this demographic, you might determine that they are interested in topics like "natural skincare," "DIY face masks," "makeup tips for beginners," "cruelty-free beauty brands," etc.

You can then use these interests as keywords in your prompt to generate relevant content for your audience. Here's an example of a prompt that uses these keywords:

> *"Could you generate a blog post providing makeup tips for beginners, specifically focusing on the use of cruelty-free beauty brands?"*

## Strike The Right Tone Of Voice

Targeting a specific audience means speaking to them in a way that appeals to them. For some groups, this might mean writing humorously and light-heartedly. For other groups, it might mean adopting a more professional demeanor and tone. For others, it could mean writing about a subject matter as though you are an expert in it while retaining a friendly and approachable attitude. If you want to hit the right tone of voice for your audience in your writing, you must specify that in your prompt.

If you're especially struggling with landing on the exact tone of voice and style that you want, the one thing you can do is find an article or piece of writing that has nailed that tone and style. You can then provide that piece of writing to ChatGPT as a sample. Of course, you'll have to follow a formula to do this. Once you've found your writing sample, fire up ChatGPT and type something like:

> *"The text in {} is a writing sample. Please ingest it as a description of the desired writing style"* or something of the sort (Gonzales, 2023).

Feel free to point out exactly which elements from the writing style—directness, satire, level of detail, etc.—you want in ChatGPT's response, then review it carefully to see if it did get the style and tone you were looking for. If not, further define the elements in the writing sample that you want ChatGPT to use and keep going until you're satisfied with what you have. Use different samples to train ChatGPT in different writing styles if you can.

As you develop descriptions you like, save them somewhere, like a document on your computer, to use as *Priming Prompts* for next time. For the record, a *priming prompt* is the first command you give to ChatGPT to establish the context.

## Optimize Prompts Using ChatGPT Special Features

You can leverage a selection of distinctive features in ChatGPT to enhance your prompts even more.

### Utilize Prefixes:

Think of a prefix as a 'mood-setter' for your conversation with ChatGPT. It's a way of giving it a hint about the kind of response you're expecting. For example, if you prefix your question with:

*"Once upon a time,"*

ChatGPT will understand that you're asking for a story-like response. Another example might be:

*"List the top 10..."*

### Adjust Length & Temperature:

ChatGPT allows you to adjust this in the settings panel or preferences. *Length,* as you know, refers to the number of words and characters the response will have. *Temperature* denotes the level of creativity or randomness found in them. If you're uncertain about how creative you want the response to be, playing around with different temperature settings might be a good idea. You can then read through your responses and choose the one you like best.

### Explore Different Formats:

ChatGPT has two formats for you to choose from. These formats are *sentence completions* and *open-ended questions.* Sentence completions are exactly what they sound like. They're prompts that begin with something like:

*"Strength training is very important for your cardiovascular health because...".*

Open-ended questions are conversation starters. They're questions that don't have simple "yes" or "no" answers but require further explanations, such as:

*"What are the cardiovascular benefits of strength training?"*

*"How does the gut microbiome affect cognitive functioning?"*

*"How can you tell when someone has a crush on you?"*

## Receive Text-Based Feedback:

Remember how ChatGPT learns from human feedback? Well, in addition to that, it can also give you feedback on your prompts. This feature is called Text-Based Feedback, which you can use to improve your prompts. Write something like:

*"How can I refine my previous prompt?"*

## Use Suggested Prompts:

Alternatively, ChatGPT can suggest prompts for you. You can then use these prompts as is or tweak them so they're closer to what you want. Either way, you'll save some time and energy.

## Use Text Tokens:

Imagine text tokens as helpful friends that step in to prevent errors, keep your project fresh and updated and help you save a lot of tedious work. Say that you are working on a long project, and halfway through, you decide to change the main character's name. By now, you have used that name in your project several times. You have two options: Go through the entire work and find the spots where the name is used to actively change it, or use text tokens to update the name everywhere. Unless you have masochistic tendencies—no judgment if you do—you will likely be better off going with the latter. This is what that can look like:

**Prompt:** *I've changed the main character's name from Jake to David.*

**ChatGPT:** *Noted. From now on, I will refer to the main character as David. How can I assist you further?*

And voila... The machine does its thing; you can sit and relax.

# Key Takeaways

- To make effective prompts for ChatGPT, use a clear context, be specific, and refine your question step by step.

- For personalized answers, tell ChatGPT to play a role, like saying, "You are a cardiologist..."

- If you want to control how creative or random the responses are, change the temperature settings.

- To prevent answers from being cut off, adjust the text length. Or, you can simply ask ChatGPT to "continue with your answer."

- If you need more precise answers, break your questions into smaller parts.

- Think about who you're talking to and use words and a tone that matches them. This way, your content will be just right for your audience.

- If you want to make your prompts better, text-based feedback can help.

- Keep checking and tweaking your prompts based on what you get back until you're happy with them.

# Test Your Knowledge

**1. Which of the following best describes one of the 3 Golden Rules for effective prompt engineering?**
   a) Always ask questions in a casual, clear tone
   b) Be specific in your question to get the desired answer much faster
   c) Repeat the question until you get the correct answer

**2. What can you do to overcome the text being occasionally cut off?**
   a) Ignore the cut-off text and continue with the next query
   b) Break down your queries into smaller bits
   c) Adjust the maximum text length setting

**3. How can you use prefixes with ChatGPT to enhance your prompts?**
   a) Prefixes act as a 'mood-setter' for your conversation with ChatGPT
   b) Prefixes are used to adjust the temperature setting of a response

c) Prefixes are specifically for changing character names in stories

**4. Let's say that you have to write a scientific article about how your gut microbiome contributes to Alzheimer's and how it can be used as a possible treatment for it. Which prompt sent to ChatGPT will yield the best results?**

a) Tell me about Alzheimer's and the gut microbiome

b) In the context of Alzheimer's, how does the gut microbiome influence the disease progression, and what are the potential treatment implications?

c) Can you provide some information about the relationship between the gut microbiome and Alzheimer's disease?

Answers: 1-b, 2-c, 3-a, 4-b

Now that you have mastered the art of crafting prompts, let's explore the real-world applications of ChatGPT and how you can put your newfound skills to work.

## Chapter Four

# The ChatGPT Effect & How AI Is Shaping The Future Of Work

*"There is no reason and no way that a human mind can keep up with an artificial intelligence machine by 2035."*

Gray Scott

Artificial intelligence has long been part of our lives in the information age. In recent years, many things that used to be part of the sci-fi world have become part of our reality and new normal. Still, the staggering speed with which artificial intelligence gained momentum is startling to think about. What's more startling is how much it has changed in our lives in just a short amount of time. These days you can use AI to achieve any number of things, from drawing mesmerizing pictures to writing entire novels and more. This being the case, speculation has been running rampant as to how AI—and, more specifically, ChatGPT—will alter the nature of work itself. There is no question that ChatGPT will give rise to some massive changes in work culture, regardless of industry, but what will that change look like?

# ChatGPT In Marketing & Advertising

ChatGPT has rapidly transformed marketing and advertising in recent years, accelerating campaigns and improving the targeting of the right audiences. These changes have greatly benefited many brands and companies. The transformation has been achieved by introducing a number of innovations; for example, ChatGPT has made email marketing services much faster and more effective by generating creative campaign prompts (Tanya, 2023).

These prompts have proven instrumental in helping businesses improve their email marketing strategies. They have also caused subscriber engagement to rise substantially, and no wonder. Thanks to ChatGPT, email marketing is far more personalized than it used to be. It is not that marketers couldn't personalize emails in previous email campaigns, of course. It is that doing so would have taken them an endless amount of time, causing them—or rather the interns they would task with this duty—to give up in short order. Put simply, then, ChatGPT has made email marketing a lot more efficient with minimal effort.

That is one of many changes it has brought to email campaigns. It has also segmented audiences, ensuring that only those interested in what is being said receive the emails in question, which is another reason why subscriber engagement has increased in email marketing.

Add to that the fact that ChatGPT uses technology to analyze language and create content that perfectly matches the preferences and tone expected by each recipient. The benefits ChatGPT offers to this marketing segment become all too clear.

Yet email marketing isn't the only segment that has benefitted from AI. Social media marketers can now enhance their content creation too. ChatGPT allows them to generate content far more efficiently and effectively than was previously possible, no matter the social media platform.

Moreover, the benefits extend beyond mere time-saving. It has revolutionized their content writing by infusing fresh and innovative ideas, opening up unexplored perspectives, and offering more polished ways to articulate their thoughts. This transformation in content creation has not only streamlined the process but has elevated the overall quality of their work.

Like with email marketing, it has increased viewer interaction as well. How could it not, when it has been finding the best hashtags to use in seconds, generating wholly original captions, finding new influencers in various niches to engage with, and writing posts that near-instantly go viral (Tuvar, 2023)? ChatGPT has even been writing copy for social media ads, which certainly has some exciting implications for the future of social media marketers.

Another field of marketing that ChatGPT has influenced is product description. ChatGPT has truly revolutionized product descriptions, making creating fascinating, entertaining, and informative ones ridiculously easy. In the process, it has all but done away with the concept of writer's block, at least where copywriters are concerned. It certainly has done away with sub-par product descriptions that are too vague to understand or that misrepresent the product they are describing.

And that's not all. One of the most significant benefits ChatGPT has offered to product description is that it has been able to craft ones that truly understand and thus address the target audience. Undoubtedly, this has impacted customer engagement and sales themselves. It has built emotional connection with customers through these simple descriptions and called them to action through the power of language alone. That, right there, is a frightening ability when you think about it, which is why it is not surprising to see ChatGPT influencing the field of journalism and content creation either.

# ChatGPT In Journalism & Content Creation

The idea of using ChatGPT for writing, be it journalistic or related to content creation, might sound a little strange at first. However, the more you think about it, the more it makes sense. ChatGPT can be incredibly useful in writing. In fact, these days, it can be used to write poems, stories, and even entire novels. This doesn't mean that ChatGPT will replace the journalists, authors, and content creators of the world, of course. It just means that it can and will play a more significant role in their endeavor to create.

Take journalism. A journalist's job is a hefty one, where they have to constantly look for news, ask the right kinds of questions, make meticulous observations, fact check, fact check, and fact check. Part of their job is intuition, since they have to, at times, sniff out stories and get the scoop, to use an old-time cliché. The thing is, this can be really hard to do in the age that we live in. So much keeps happening in the span of a single day; so much information is being exchanged in a mere hour that you sometimes feel like you're drowning in data, even if you're not a journalist. So, how do you sort through all that information and find exactly what you're looking for? This is where ChatGPT comes to the fore.

You see, ChatGPT is capable of sifting through an immense amount of data ridiculously quickly and efficiently (Abdulrahman, 2023). Let's face it, no journalist can rival it in this arena, no matter how exceptional they are. Not only can ChatGPT sift through mountains of data very quickly, but it can also provide invaluable insights about ongoing or emerging trends. A good journalist can then use this information to craft an intriguing news article or write an op-ed. They can use these data points to generate interesting interview questions too. Naturally, ChatGPT can help with this process, contributing its own set of questions relevant to the interview subject. This way, a journalist can generate unexpected questions that others might not have asked in previous interviews and craft a really entertaining piece to read.

Similarly, ChatGPT can help them to generate eye-catching headlines and titles for their articles and the like. Writing a title that accurately encompasses what an article is about and is still catchy and memorable can be challenging. At times, a journalist might find it harder to do than writing the actual article. However, if they were to put their main data points into ChatGPT, they'd be able to accomplish this in record time. They could even make sure that their headlines are search engine optimized (SEO) as they're being written.

Journalists often have to read a lot of articles and news pieces written by others to keep up to date on current events. This is a task that's as necessary as it is time-consuming. Luckily, ChatGPT can help them in this avenue too. ChatGPT is excellent at going through hundreds of news articles and summarizing them with their key highlights pointed out. It can even give you a shorter version of the summaries it provides you with, as well as re-write it in its entirety or pick out specific info from it. That this is an immensely useful feature for journalists, both for research and quoting purposes, is obvious.

The one ChatGPT feature that might possibly beat this one is its fact-checking capability. Since ChatGPT can go through massive amounts of text in seconds, it can also fact-check the articles a journalist writes in seconds. It can rapidly find and point out any inaccuracies, allowing the journalist to correct them before their work is published, which does wonders for one's credibility. A last golden feature ChatGPT can offer newspaper men and women across the globe is its translation feature. The AI can translate pretty much any language into any other language.

Now, don't think it's all about journalists. ChatGPT can be very useful for anyone looking to create content, from blog writers to content marketers. For example, that summary feature? That can easily be used to summarize an entire book, which will come in very handy for college students who have to pull an all-nighter to write up their book reports. The fact-checking feature, too, can save a content marketer in a pinch, especially if it prevents them from publishing an article riddled with inaccuracies.

Finally, regardless of what kind of writer you are, ChatGPT can help you draft outlines, which can be a curiously tricky thing, especially if you struggle with organizing your thoughts. Those outlines can be as detailed or brief and general as you'd like them to be. That is true so long as you clarify what you want in your prompt. In addition, ChatGPT can proofread and optimize your writing to reach the right audience. In this respect, ChatGPT is one of your biggest marketing tools.

## ChatGPT In Education & E-Learning

Another area ChatGPT proves its usefulness is education and e-learning. Just ask today's high school and college students, and even their teachers. From a teacher's perspective, ChatGPT can whittle down their obscenely heavy workload. For all that they're under-compensated and underappreciated, teachers do a stupefying amount of work. When not grading homework, they're prepping for the following day's course, creating PowerPoint presentations for class, planning field trips, and more. One of the most tedious things that they have to do, though, is preparing quizzes.

Preparing quizzes is tedious because you have to create new ones every time—you can't plagiarize your own work from last year, sadly. You have to find new ways to test your students' knowledge and ability to use what they've learned. This can be really hard, as anyone who has ever had to prepare a survey, quiz, or even a mock interview knows. Thankfully, ChatGPT can ease this burden by generating questions for you. If you want it to be able to do this, though, you have to feed as specific a prompt as you can. That prompt should include your question, whether it should be a multiple choice question, how many questions you want it to write like that, and more (Ogulcan, n.d.). As always, once ChatGPT has responded, you can have that response further refined by tweaking your original prompt.

When generating such quiz questions, though, you need to remember that, by OpenAI's own admission, the platform's general knowledge of current events that happened post-2021 is rather limited (Nguyen, 2023). So, if your quiz questions have to do with post-2021 events, you may struggle just a tiny bit.

As for the student's side, ChatGPT can answer exam and quiz questions. Of course, this won't do much good for exams and quizzes they take at school, but for take-at-home tests and online ones? Well, it could be a good trick for students to keep up their sleeves.

Another way in which ChatGPT can be very useful to both students and teachers is by providing them with summaries of study materials. For students, this is useful for studying and reviewing, especially before big exams. This goes doubly for any books they have had to read—and by that, I mean pretended to have read—for their English classes.

Now, ChatGPT can be a great study buddy in more ways than one. For instance, if you're struggling to memorize information before a test, like important dates or equations, you can ask ChatGPT to come up with a good song or rhyme that can help you remember them. You can ask it to prepare sample questions, much like your teachers would prepare quiz questions on it. Thus, you can obtain a practice test or two and work your way through them.

On top of all that, ChatGPT can be a big help with note-taking. It's like having a personal assistant to jot down and keep track of information on any subject you can think of. All you have to do is provide ChatGPT with a prompt explaining what you want it to take notes on. Once it has prepared your notes, you can have it organize and label them, so you know exactly where to find different bites of information.

Moreover, one of the biggest struggles that a typical student faces is planning and time management. This is why teachers often encourage students to create study plans for themselves. Unfortunately, it can be challenging to do, if you don't know how to go about it. Enter ChatGPT, as always. A great way to have it begin crafting a study plan for you is to provide it with your exam and quiz dates, the dates when your semesters begin and end, and the different sets of subjects you need to study at different times. If your teachers were foreseeing enough to provide you with syllabi, then feed the information there to ChatGPT. Once it has all the data it needs, it can create a study plan and schedule that works for you. If you feel you need to focus a little more on, say, math rather than history when studying, make sure to tell that to ChatGPT, and it will alter your study plan to reflect this need.

Additionally, if you're a student, you're bound to be given homework. Typically, students are either given essay assignments or worksheets. If you have an essay due, ChatGPT can help you to come up with ideas to write about, check your spelling and grammar, and even help to cite sources, which can be irritatingly tedious when you have to do it alone. Furthermore, it can help you to fact-check your homework, be it an essay or a worksheet you just completed. If you're stuck on a particular problem or are having trouble understanding why it's solved the way it is, then one thing you can do is enter it into ChatGPT. You can then ask it to provide you with step-by-step instructions and explain how it's solved. This way, not only will you get good marks on your homework, but you'll be sure that you really understand what you're learning.

Lastly, one of the best parts of ChatGPT is the personalized learning experience it can provide you with. To take advantage of this capability, you'll have to share things like your quiz and exam scores and answers, writing samples, and sample homework with ChatGPT. The AI will then be able to thoroughly analyze the data it has been provided with. Based on the conclusions it arrives at, it'll be able to identify gaps in your knowledge, things you need a little more help getting right, and the best ways of reinforcing what you know. Using that knowhow, it'll be able to create personalized recommendations for you on what you should read and review, alongside practice exercises that will help you, and suggested learning materials.

Of course, ChatGPT isn't just good for students, as you've seen. Going back to the teachers' end of things, it's easy to see just how helpful it can be for them. Take grading, which can be just as tedious and tiring an endeavor as creating quizzes and exams can be. Nowadays, this is a responsibility that a teacher can take off their shoulders and place on ChatGPT's virtual ones (Ohiri, 2023). This works best with things like multiple-choice questions and queries that require answers that are on the shorter side. By putting students' exam and quiz papers through ChatGPT, you can easily grade them in minutes, rather than spend hours and hours doing it yourself.

ChatGPT can be incorporated into academic life outside of the classroom as well. These days, many universities use it to provide students with a chatbot that can help them navigate the campus register for their different courses, and even get internship and career advice. Also, some professors integrate ChatGPT into the digital textbooks they use, thereby creating an interactive learning environment for their students. This allows them to interject videos, pop-ups, examples, and more into the course materials, enhancing their students' learning experience. Add to that how ChatGPT can be used as a kind of virtual tutoring method outside of class, and a point can be made about how ChatGPT can become the future of e-learning, at least to a degree.

# ChatGPT In Software Development

ChatGPT can benefit many different fields, but nowhere is its benefit more evident than in software development and data science. Odds are, one of the first words that pops into your head when you hear "ChatGPT" is "developer." How could that not be the case when lines and lines of code had to have been used to create ChatGPT in the first place? Nowadays, though, the relationship between ChatGPT and coding isn't just one-way. Just as coding was used to create ChatGPT, ChatGPT can be used to write lines of code.

For those of you that are new to the world of coding, think of it like speaking different languages in different countries. Just as you might speak French in France and Spanish in Spain, developers use various coding languages such as Python, JavaScript, C#, and Java. These languages are the tools developers use to "talk" to computers and create different programs and applications. Now, imagine ChatGPT as a well-traveled polyglot who's fluent in all these coding languages. Today, ChatGPT can create code snippets in all these languages and more. It can even do more specialized tasks like creating sample comma-separated value (CSV) inputs, which are used to solve real-world challenges like data science problems or crafting infrastructure templates as code.

Now, If you've ever tried your hand at writing code, you know how lengthy and arduous a process it can be. Place a single dot somewhere it's not supposed to be, or accidentally hit space when writing your code, and at best, the app or whatever else you were developing will have annoying glitches. You'll then need to comb through the entire code you have written, possibly with a magnifying glass, so you can find and remove that typo causing all your problems. This is the main headache that ChatGPT can spare you because, unlike us mere humans, AI won't make such minuscule errors. It will accurately generate the code you need and do it ten times as fast as you could ever hope to.

An additional benefit of using ChatGPT to generate code is that it can introduce you to alternative ways of doing this. Remember those cliché sitcom scenes where a child asks a parent for help with math homework? The parent, confident at first, tries to explain the old way they learned, only for the child to shake their head and say, *"That's not how we're supposed to do it."* The child then shows the new method, leaving the parent baffled and saying, *"I don't understand this new math,"* before giving up. Well, coding is a bit like that. It constantly evolves with new methods and approaches, sometimes leaving even seasoned developers scratching their heads. ChatGPT comes into play here like a tech-savvy kid who's up to date with the latest coding 'math.' If you find yourself stuck like that bewildered parent, you can turn to ChatGPT, which will introduce you to new ways of doing things. So, instead of walking away confused, you can learn and grow with ChatGPT as your modern coding buddy.

Speaking of debugging, this is another matter you can use ChatGPT in (Dilmegani, 2023). Say that you've encountered an error message and have no idea what typo that error stems from. Just fire up ChatGPT and insert code snippets into it, then ask it to analyze and suggest possible fixes for them. That sounds much easier than going over your code with a fine-tooth comb, doesn't it? Alternatively, say that you've been working on a code for who knows how long. You have a deadline, but you're downright exhausted. You need sleep, but if you give into that need, you won't be able to finish your code. In this case, you can turn to ChatGPT - which can predict what the next lines in your code are supposed to be based on the already-existing ones. This process can also reduce any possible mistakes you may make when coding.

ChatGPT is capable of yet another coding-related feat, which is code refactoring. That's a fancy word for saying that it can improve your code's readability, structure, and overall quality. Think of code refactoring as editing. If this were an actual book you're writing, then code refactoring would be the edits your editor—ChatGPT—gave you. ChatGPT can provide you with these editorial notes in a number of ways. It can suggest changes for variable names, remove redundant bits of code, and suggest other improvements.

There's one last thing ChatGPT can do for you where coding is concerned, and that's code documentation. Basically, ChatGPT can recommend certain ready templates for you to use, depending on what you want your code to accomplish. If you're unsure of which template to use, it can make suggestions and examples, even going as far as to explain complex-looking codes to you.

## ChatGPT In Data Science

We live in a world where we're swimming up to our eyeballs in data. Some of this data is superfluous, while other data is very important and useful. This is doubly true for anyone whose job entails analyzing the copious amounts of data they're given every day—like those who have to make market analyses. Such individuals have to wade through this vast pool of data and find the information they need while weeding through the rest. Doing this alone can be maddeningly time-consuming, but doing it with the help of ChatGPT? Not so much!

ChatGPT can be incredibly useful in data analysis thanks to its Natural Language Processing (NLP) capabilities. As we discussed early in the book, this technology enables the machine to understand and interpret human language. Imagine it as a translator between complex data and plain English. It can easily find and extract the relevant information you need and identify errors in your collected data. Then it can sort the relevant and correct ones into the proper categories, taking care to label them accurately

(Great Learning Staff, 2023). That done, it can translate raw data needing interpretation into cohesive, comprehensible narratives. Put simply, it can use what it has found and gathered to create a story or an analytics report, if you want to be a little more boring about it. These stories can immediately point out key performance indicators (KPIs) and metrics, illustrate the data's patterns, and explain them neatly and thoroughly.

ChatGPT doesn't have to just stop there, of course. It can take things a step further by identifying all relevant trends, making predictions about future ones, and coming up with plausible hypotheses. You can use these things to both plan your next moves in whatever industry you're in and ask the right insightful questions you need to analyze things further. This whole process is known as exploratory data analysis (EDA), and it goes hand in hand with something called predictive modeling. Predictive modeling means creating models for how things will turn out in the future. ChatGPT can assist with this, too, by giving you accurate and reliable interpretations of the data and facts. It can offer you advice and guidance on determining the parameters of the model you're devising and even choose the right machine-learning algorithm that'll allow you to meet the goals you want.

Having said that, data scientists need to take the conclusions and predictions that ChatGPT makes with a grain of salt. This is because ChatGPT can be biased, depending on what kind of information and sources it has been trained on, as you already know. It's also because understanding how ChatGPT arrived at some of the conclusions it presents can be difficult. As a general rule, if a conclusion that ChatGPT presents you with is hard to understand, asking for further explanation is a good idea.

# Key Takeaways

- ChatGPT is revolutionizing marketing, adding personal touches and efficiency to campaigns.

- Journalists now use ChatGPT for data sifting, insights into trends, fact-checking, and more.

- ChatGPT allows content creators to summarize, proofread, and outline writings more effectively.

- Email marketing was transformed with ChatGPT, leading to faster, highly personalized campaigns.

- ChatGPT enhances content creation, optimizing hashtags and sparking viral posts on social media.

- Teachers benefit from ChatGPT by easing quiz creation and grading, improving time management.

- Students engage ChatGPT for personalized study plans, homework aid, and unique learning experiences.

- Software developers rely on ChatGPT for precise debugging, analyzing, and fixing of code.

- ChatGPT generates accurate and speedy code, avoiding typical human errors in development.

- In data analysis, ChatGPT translates complex data into plain English, crafting insightful narratives.

Before we move on, let's put all the knowledge you've gathered to the test. Up next, I've got two real-world scenarios for you. Think of it as a hands-on workshop tucked right inside these pages. You'll get to apply what you've learned and tackle some challenges head-on. Ready? Let's get started!

# Test Your Knowledge

## Case Study #1:

You've just been appointed as the head of the e-learning department at a progressive university. The university administration is eager to incorporate cutting-edge AI technologies to enhance both the teaching and learning experience. You've learned that ChatGPT can be a game-changer in education, but you need to devise a concrete plan to implement it efficiently. Your challenges are multifaceted. The faculty needs assistance in grading, quiz creation, and enhancing their teaching materials, while the students require support in studying, note-taking, planning, homework assistance, and personalized learning experiences.

**1. How would you use ChatGPT to assist faculty members in grading multiple-choice questions and short answers efficiently, without losing the personal touch that human graders can provide?**

a) Have ChatGPT grade all papers without any human intervention and leave personalized comments on each student's performance

b) Implement ChatGPT to grade the objective parts of the exam, like multiple-choice questions, while teachers manually grade subjective answers and add personal feedback

c) Use ChatGPT only for generating quiz questions, but not for grading, leaving all the assessment responsibilities to the teachers

**2. The students are struggling with time management and study planning. How would you deploy ChatGPT to aid them in crafting a personalized study plan?**

a) Ask students to manually input all of their subjects, quiz dates, and personal preferences into a system, and then have ChatGPT generate a one-size-fits-all study plan

b) Leave study planning to students without any AI assistance, and focus only on ChatGPT's ability to help with note-taking

c) Encourage students to share their exam scores, quiz dates, subject preferences, and specific learning needs with ChatGPT, allowing it to analyze the data and create a tailored study plan that reflects individual needs

Answers: 1-b, 2-c

## Case Study #2:

You've joined the customer service team of a brand-new meditation app. At present, you're the only customer service member on board. People use the app all the time, including late at night and on the weekends, and because the app is new, many glitches must be fixed. The technical team is on it, and it's up to you to keep them informed of the situation and to let the technical team know what issues customers are experiencing. Yet, you are only a single individual. You need rest and sleep, which means you cannot report all night, every night and through the weekends.

**1. How can you use ChatGPT to manage the situation of customers reporting issues at all hours?**

a) I can develop and deploy new features based on user feedback overnight

b) I can use it to draft and send personalized emails to every customer, addressing their concerns

c) I can use it to create an automated system that collects user issues and creates a report for the technical team

**2. Since constant reporting to the technical team is indispensable, how can ChatGPT assist you with this while you rest?**

a) By analyzing the app's glitches and automatically deploying fixes to the server

b) By monitoring user feedback and summarizing the most common problems for me to report

c) By engaging with customers on social media to gather insights and promote the app

Now you're working in the development team of the same meditation app. Recently, you and your team released an update for the app, which immediately started crashing...

**3. How can ChatGPT assist the development team in identifying the error?**

a) By generating code snippets and potential scenarios that could have caused the bug

b) By analyzing user behavior and proposing possible solutions based on their feedback

c) By translating the app's content into different languages to expand its global reach

**4. How might ChatGPT be used to not only fix the existing bug but also to enhance the overall quality of the code?**

a) By conducting a detailed analysis of user reviews and proposing new app features

b) By collaborating with the design team to create a new visual identity for the app, with a simpler code to avoid future crashes

c) By providing code examples, best practices and suggestions for improvements to the existing code

Answers: 1-c, 2-b, 3-a, 4-c

## Chapter Five

# Your Impact In The AI Revolution

"Knowledge sharing is a cost we can all cover, and one that society can't afford to neglect."

Unknown

In our ever-changing world, many folks struggle to keep up with the fast pace. But what if we all had a chance to get ahead? It could be as simple as learning something new and getting better at what we do.

So, why aren't more of us jumping on this opportunity? Well, sometimes it's hard to know where to start or what to learn. That's where you and I come in.

With your help, we can spread the insights in this book and invite more people into the exciting realm of AI and ChatGPT. It's about making connections, creating opportunities, and sharing the knowledge that can change lives.

I've done the initial work here, and now I'm reaching out to you as a friend. Would you spare one minute of your time? By posting a review of this book on Amazon, you'll be like a guiding star for those looking to find their way.

Yes, it's as simple as that. A short review of what you think so far, or even a star rating of this book on Amazon, will greatly help other people unfamiliar with this new technology.

Scan the QR code to leave a quick review and join me in this incredible journey of helping others.

Thank you!

## Chapter Six

# ChatGPT's Powerful Impact In The Workforce

*"Just as electricity transformed almost everything 100 years ago, today, I actually have a hard time thinking of an industry that I don't think AI will transform in the next several years."*

Andrew Ng

Since ChatGPT impacts various industries, it also impacts the workforce that's part of them. Fact of the matter is that the various features and services that ChatGPT offers are redefining people's job descriptions. With the rate things are progressing, teachers might not even have to grade exams soon. Customer service professionals these days don't have to interact with customers as much. If ChatGPT progresses just a little more, there might come a time when they don't have to interact with them in real life ever again. There may similarly come a time when journalists and content creators rely heavily on AI to edit and proofread their works, rather than on their editors and publishers. So, what do all these various changes mean for the future of different industries, and how will they transform the workforce of the world?

# ChatGPT In Healthcare

The healthcare industry is arguably one of the biggest industries in the world, if not the biggest. This is more than understandable. After all, everyone needs or will need proper healthcare at some point in their lives. According to the World Health Organization (WHO), the global healthcare industry was valued at $8.45 trillion in 2018 alone (Kesherim, 2023). How exactly has ChatGPT affected an industry so large and impactful, then?

There have been attempts to introduce AI into healthcare in the past, but it was slow going. This changed with the COVID-19 pandemic, when people were stuck at home and couldn't go to the ER for fear of getting sick, even when they needed medical help. So, telemedicine was introduced into the picture, and ChatGPT played a significant role in this. Telemedicine allows patients to seek medical advice and treatment via phone and virtual assistants (Moore, 2023). These virtual assistants, created with AI, do everything from helping patients book appointments to managing their healthcare information. Today healthcare professionals rely quite a bit on AI, particularly where telemedicine is concerned, because it can aid in the clinical decisions they must make. Though ultimately, your human doctor will always be the one to make a call about your condition and prescribe you something, ChatGPT can be heavily involved in the process. It can help with the diagnosis by making real-time recommendations based on the evidence at hand. It can spot and flag potential drug interactions too, saving patients and doctors a lot of hassle later on.

Given ChatGPT's recall abilities, it's understandable that it would also be amazing at medical record-keeping. From summarizing the medical histories of countless patients to streamlining the record-keeping process, it has a lot to offer the healthcare industry in this arena. One way in which this feature could be leveraged in the future is through dictation.

Assuming voice-to-text technologies advance sufficiently (which they will) then doctors will be able to dictate their findings, test results, symptoms, and more to ChatGPT. ChatGPT can then summarize the key information and use that to make extrapolations.

This technology does more than keep efficient records; it also makes things easier to understand for patients. As often happens, getting a diagnosis can sometimes be a rather confusing thing for them. This is because said diagnosis might be riddled with medical terms and test results that they don't really understand—how could they, seeing as they probably never attended medical school? In such a case, a patient will usually go to Google, which will take some time and effort, seeing as they'll have to read and look up a lot. With ChatGPT, though, they won't have to. Instead, they can translate the medical language into layman's terms, thus getting a decent understanding of their own diagnosis and treatment.

Likewise, they can have these things translated into other languages, like Chinese and Spanish, which is essential, seeing as not everyone speaks the same primary language.

While the immediate benefits to patients regarding understanding are clear, there is also a broader potential application for AI in more complex and innovative medical scenarios.

In particular, ChatGPT really comes to the fore in the arena of clinical trials. The various capabilities that it has, which we have covered so far, can be vital to developing new treatment methods. Furthermore, they can be utilized to develop new diagnostic tools, find the best willing participants for trials, check symptoms, keep track of participants' progress, and more. Medical professionals can then use all this to alter treatments, work on the newer iterations of trials, and determine the next steps. Later on, this information can be leveraged for educational purposes.

Actually, as in e-learning, ChatGPT can be used to further the education of both medical students and medical professionals like doctors and surgeons. Medicine is an ever-evolving field, with new drugs, treatments, and approaches being invented daily. A medical professional needs to keep up to date with all these things, which means they constantly have to keep furthering their education. Only then can they be sure they are providing their patients with the most current and best possible care.

It must be remembered, however, that "care" doesn't just mean pre-scribing someone the right drugs in the medical field. It also means taking care of their mental health and well-being. ChatGPT can help with this by providing patients with mental health support, checking on their well-being post-treatment, and monitoring them. It can keep track of disease progression and development and help with medication management. In doing so, it can ensure that every aspect of patient care is well and truly covered.

The one hang-up with all of this is that ChatGPT isn't quite as empa-thetic as it can be when interacting with patients, at least not compared to human doctors and healthcare professionals. This, however, is only a momentary issue (*Will ChatGPT Transform Healthcare?*, 2023). Chat-GPT is currently being trained to be more empathetic in its dialogue and responses, which means it will get better over time. Once it does, the things it offers the healthcare industry will be limitless, especially since it will significantly increase the healthcare coverage that doctors can provide their patients with.

## ChatGPT In Entertainment

The idea of using ChatGPT and AI in general, in a creative field like the entertainment industry, might sound a little foreign. However, it's neither as unusual nor as uncommon as you might expect. These days, a staggering amount of people use ChatGPT for entertainment purposes, be it to write a poem or story, create comedic skits for an open-mic night, or even come up with script ideas for TV shows, movies, and plays (Saeed, 2023).

Actually, many people, including big shots in Hollywood, use ChatGPT to come up with new ideas. To do this, they feed existing scripts similar to the kind of work they want to create, such as a romantic comedy, thriller, or whatever else. They train ChatGPT on these models, which constitute the dataset it's given, if you feel like getting a bit technical about things. In this way, ChatGPT learns exactly what format and style it's supposed to use, as well as stuff like how to build tension in a plot, do character development, weave a climactic ending, and more.

Say you're part of a studio that's looking for the next big TV show idea. ChatGPT can make this quest of yours far easier to accomplish, seeing as it can generate a ton of ideas in record time. Later on, you can pick one idea from the options it presents you with. Alternatively, you can refine your prompt to specify exactly what kind of script you're looking for, so that ChatGPT gives you other ideas that might be a better fit for what you have in mind.

Of course, the entertainment industry doesn't just mean movies and TV shows. It encompasses video games, skits, stand-up routines, music, poetry, books, and comic books. An argument can be made that pick-up lines—the ones that aren't clichéd, at least—and personalized responses for virtual assistants are also considered part of the entertainment sphere. If you've ever played video games, particularly the role-playing and action varieties, you know that they're heavy on the big, arching storylines, multiple endings with multiple choices, and intriguing dialogue. Essentially, a good video game is a bit like a novel or movie you can play, and writing one of those can be hard. This is doubly true for scenes where dialogue between your character and the non-playable characters unfolds and changes depending on your choices. Fortunately, ChatGPT can lend you a hand when you're crafting these dialogue branches. As before, you'll need to train ChatGPT on game dialogue conventions. Only then will it be able to create the kinds of dialogue pathways you're looking for.

Remember how you could use ChatGPT to create a song when studying so that you can remember various facts more easily? Well, the poems and songs that ChatGPT helps you with do not have to be for educational purposes only. They can be poems you just want to write for creativity's sake, too. So long as you train ChatGPT on copious amounts of poetry, it can learn the model and style you want and start writing ones of its own in no time. The same goes for song lyrics. Using ChatGPT like this is an excellent way of coming up with some original materials to use. You don't have to use the poems and lyrics exactly as ChatGPT made them, either. You can use the AI's work as a sort of template and then get to work playing around with the text at hand. Thus, you can create a collaborative work with ChatGPT that's no less creative and beautiful than any other work out there.

Considering all these different examples of how ChatGPT affects creative work, you cannot help but wonder how AI is going to affect storytelling in its many forms in the future. Some people, for instance, are worried that the use of AI in storytelling will result in a loss of original content (AIContentfy Team, 2023). "*Won't AI continually keep producing the same kind of materials over and over again?*", they ask. The thing is, though, the kind of content ChatGPT creates depends entirely on what you train it on and how you word your prompt. These two things are bound to change from person to person, which means that ChatGPT is bound to receive different kinds of inputs from different people. Doesn't it stand to reason, then, that its output will always be different as well?

Another concern some people have raised is how AI will impact storytellers' role in creative industries. *"Is it possible that ChatGPT, for example, will be able to replace novelists or screenwriters? If so, wouldn't that dramatically affect the livelihoods of novelists, screenwriters and the like?"* To be fair, this is a valid question to voice, but it's too soon to tell whether AI will actually replace storytellers or not. What will most likely end up happening, though, is that storytellers and AI will fall into a more collaborative relationship, as in the poem-lyrics example previously discussed. Alternatively, creative spaces may end up accommodating both human and AI storytellers. This would be very interesting to see, since these two types of storytellers are bound to have different approaches and ways of looking at the world.

A final concern regarding storytelling and AI is that AI will be used as a tool in the creative fields to spread propaganda and misinformation. But here's the thing, while this is a reasonable worry, human beings have long been using storytelling as a misinformation and propaganda tool. Just look at the copious films Nazi Germany made back when they were in power. Human beings don't need AI to be able to use storytelling for their own purposes. AI may hasten their ability to spread propaganda, of course, but not by much, at least not in the day and age that we live in. While this concern is something to keep in mind regarding the future of storytelling, it should not be used to condemn AI's role in it.

## ChatGPT In Customer Service

If you've been in the customer service trenches before, you're well aware it can feel a bit like a spirit-crushing gig, especially when certain customers come into play. Here's where ChatGPT can swoop in as your lifeline, bringing sanity back into your work life. As we've been discussing, folks in the customer service scene are already pretty familiar with AI – chatbots have been handling FAQ-style queries for a while now. But ChatGPT takes this to a whole new ballpark.

ChatGPT lends a more human touch to responses to customers' issues and inquiries by featuring skills such as text completion, generation, and classification. And let's face it – customers appreciate this. Nobody enjoys the feeling of chatting with a cold, uncaring bot that seems oblivious to their issues. Having a conversation with a "real" entity, ready and willing to lend a hand, creates a sense of comfort and makes help seem more attainable.

Customer service reps also give ChatGPT two thumbs up for handling customer queries independently. It saves them from endlessly repeating the same replies to the same questions. With their freed-up time, they can take closer looks at more urgent messages and problems and even think up ways to improve the customer service process for everyone in the long run.

Another great benefit that ChatGPT brings to the table for both customers and customer service officials is its translation properties. Some people speak different languages, as we keep saying, and because of this, sometimes things can get lost in translation. ChatGPT can ensure that that is never the case by handling translation matters.

Furthermore, these days ChatGPT can analyze the sentiment of customer messages. In doing so, it can differentiate between a truly angry, attack-oriented message from calm and understanding one. Having made this differentiation, it can then respond in the most appropriate way. In the first case, this might require adopting an appeasing and apologetic language. In the second, it might require adopting a calmer, more friendly tone. For other kinds of messages, ChatGPT can use a language and tone entirely different from these.

That ChatGPT can respond to the sentiment with which a customer writes their message is very much in line with its ability to write personalized messages to customers. ChatGPT's responses can be tailor-made for specific customers, once it has reviewed and analyzed their specific data. While this ability is very impressive at present, it must be said that it's still in its early stages. As time goes by, it's bound to keep changing and evolving, until ChatGPT can start treating everyone it interacts with as an individual in their own right. Not to mention that it will be able to do this while retaining the tone of voice and individuality of the brand it's representing.

In conclusion, ChatGPT is transforming the landscape of customer service. Its skills facilitate better conversations and its continuous evolution promises even more improvements ahead. It's a new era for customer interaction, and we're just at the beginning.

# Key Takeaways:

- ChatGPT is transforming various industries and redefining job descriptions across sectors.

- In healthcare, ChatGPT aids in telemedicine, record-keeping, and real-time recommendations, including translating medical language.

- ChatGPT's potential in healthcare extends to clinical trials, education, and overall patient care, though empathy remains a work in progress.

- In entertainment, ChatGPT assists in creating poems, stories, scripts, and video game dialogues, often leading to collaboration with human creators.

- Concerns in entertainment include the potential loss of originality, replacement of human storytellers, and misuse for propaganda, but the reality is nuanced.

- In customer service, ChatGPT adds a human touch to responses, handles repetitive queries, and even translates between languages.

- Analyzing customer sentiment allows ChatGPT to respond appropriately, enhancing the customer experience.

- AI's role in sectors like education, journalism, and content creation is growing, altering traditional workflows.

- Some apprehensions exist regarding AI's replacement of human roles and potential ethical concerns.

- Overall, ChatGPT's influence is pervasive and holds great promise for diverse applications, with ongoing developments expected to address current limitations.

# Test Your Knowledge

Thus far, we have covered various industries in which ChatGPT can be used in some unique ways. These, however, aren't the only industries that can turn to AI. There are many others. Seeing as trying to cover all of them will take us pages upon pages, let's gamify things a bit and try to match different AI capabilities with different industries:

**1. ChatGPT can draw up actual legal contracts. Which industry will this capability be the best fit for?**
a) The subsidiary rights department of a publishing house
b) The contractual law department of a law office
c) Retail companies dealing with consumer goods
d) All of the above

**2. ChatGPT can identify patterns in past customer behavior that are indicative of fraud and apply these insights to predict future fraudulent activities. Who can make the best use of this feature?**

a) Someone who works in banking or the financial sector

b) Someone who works in the retail industry

c) Someone who works in the education industry

d) Someone who works in athletics

**3. ChatGPT can analyze large blocks of textual data to craft a list of the most-used keywords in a given sector. Who can make the best use of this information?**
a) An artist
b) A graphic designer
c) A copywriter
d) A CEO

**4. ChatGPT can be used in A/B testing to gain insights from different focus groups. Which industry can make the best use of this?**
a) Technology
b) Finance
c) Sales and Marketing
d) Beauty

Answers: 1-d, 2-a, 3-c, 4-c

Now that you understand how ChatGPT is revolutionizing various industries, let's dive deeper into how you can harness its power with hands-on tutorials and exercises in the next chapter.

## Chapter Seven

# From Theory To Practice —Tutorials & Exercises

*"Give me 6 hours to chop down a tree and I will spend the first hour sharpening the axe."*

Abraham Lincoln

By now, you're probably convinced that artificial intelligence and ChatGPT are some of the most useful tools you can ever add to your toolkit, no matter which industry you are in. Like any tool, however, they won't do you much good if you don't know how to use them.

Consider a kitchen knife: Who do you think will be able to make the best-looking and tasting food using that knife? Someone who has never cooked before, someone who knows how to cook but doesn't have any practice with it, or a Michelin-star chef? The answer to that question should be fairly obvious, even if you aren't the biggest fan of Michelin-star food—let's be honest, no one would blame you for that given how small their portions usually are.

The same logic that's found in this cooking example can easily be applied to ChatGPT and your ability to use it for your purposes. If you want to wield ChatGPT with the expertise that a Michelin-star chef would wield their knife, then what you must do is obvious: practice, practice, and practice. Practicing how to wield a tool gets to be infinitely easier, of course, if you know exactly what steps you need to take when using said tool. That being the case, let's dive into our step-by-step guide to using ChatGPT.

# Your Guide To Creating Written Content

One of the key things you can use ChatGPT for is creating content, as you have seen. So, how does this process unfold, and what do you need to do? Let's see:

## Step #1: Decide on a topic to write about.

The first thing you need to do is decide what exactly you want to write about. If you already have an idea, then that's great, and you can roll with it. If you don't, then turning to ChatGPT to brainstorm should help. Decide on a general area that you'd like to write about—such as artificial intelligence or virtual reality, for instance—then write down a full prompt in ChatGPT to start generating ideas (Chatman, 2023). For example:

> *"I want to write about virtual reality in healthcare. Can you help me think of some ways it's being used today?"*

## Step #2: Create an outline.

Now that you know what you want to write about, roll up your sleeves and create a basic outline for it. This might seem like tedious work, but you'd be amazed at how much it'll help you organize your ideas and how easy it'll make it for you to get writing (Kidd, 2023). One of the hardest things about writing is knowing where to start, after all. If you'd like, you can get ChatGPT's help to create your initial outline. This will save you a lot of time and energy, so it's an advisable thing to do.

To generate an outline, you'll have to describe what you want the basic idea of your article to be and specify which keywords—which you should identify before you start writing your outline—need to be used in it. Once you provide this information to ChatGPT in your prompt, the system will generate a response, as always. This response will include various headings and subheadings, subtopics you can discuss in your article that are related to your main idea, and outline the overall structure the article will follow.

If the outline you end up with feels too broad or vague, or if you want to change certain sub-topics or headings with others, simply alter your prompt to reflect your wishes. Keep tweaking your prompt until ChatG-PT gives you an outline that you are satisfied with. For example:

> *"I've decided to write about the use of virtual reality in health-care. I want to cover areas such as training for medical professionals, patient therapy, and medical visualization. Please create an outline for me with headings, subheadings, and key points under each, following this structure: Introduction, three main sections for each focus area, and a conclusion."*

## Step #3: Start writing.

As tempting as it might be, you cannot use ChatGPT to write the entirety of your article. This is because ChatGPT does better with short-form text as opposed to a lengthy one, as you'll recall. The best thing you can do as an excellent content creator is take the idea and outline you've obtained with ChatGPT's help and start running with it.

## Step #4: Fight against writer's block.

Writer's block is one of the most annoying obstacles you can come up against as a content creator or writer of any kind. Luckily, it's much easier to overcome these days, thanks to the existence of ChatGPT. Say that you've written most of your article but are stuck at the intro. Introductions can be notoriously difficult to write sometimes, since the question *"Where do I even begin?"* immediately takes hold of you. If you're experiencing this, you can provide ChatGPT with a prompt explaining what you want your intro to say and how you want it to be structured. Again, feel free to refine your prompt further if the intro it provides you isn't to your satisfaction. Keep going until you get one that you like and that works with the rest of your article. Here's an example:

> *"I've written most of my article about the use of virtual reality in healthcare, covering areas like training for medical professionals, patient therapy, and medical visualization. However, I'm stuck on the introduction. I want it to be engaging, provide an overview of the three main focus areas, and hint at the transformative impact of virtual reality in the medical field. Please help me craft an introduction that fits this criteria."*

## Step #5: Write your meta-descriptions.

Meta-descriptions are very important for content creators, because a really well-written one can immediately draw readers' attention and make them click on the article link. Have you ever bought a book because you read a very good quote from it, or seen a movie because of one line from one review? It's a bit like that. Writing a captivating meta-description can be a challenge, though, seeing as you're given a very limited character count for it. Meta-descriptions can only be 155 characters long, which is shorter than what Twitter allows you for a good tweet, mind you. For ChatGPT, though, that's not really the case. So long as you're specific about your wants and needs in your prompt, it'll be able to generate some fascinating meta-descriptions for your article in no time. Here's how you can go about it:

*"I need a captivating meta-description that's within 155 characters to entice my readers. It should highlight the innovative aspect of virtual reality in healthcare. Please help me craft this meta-description. Provide 5 different samples for me to choose from."*

## Step #6: Craft your social media posts.

While you're on your meta-description, you might also want to consider what you want to write about your article in your social media posts. Like an intriguing meta-description, a good tweet, post, or thread can bring a lot of readers to your article. Again, like a meta-description, writing one might be challenging. If you're struggling with this, you should look no further than ChatGPT and use it to your heart's content.

The key thing to remember when using ChatGPT as a content creator is that it's your ally and your friend, not your competition and certainly not your replacement. That means that rather than approaching it with wariness, you should freely add it to your toolkit and use it to become even better at your job than you already are. For example:

*"Based on all the information you have regarding my article, please help me create engaging posts for platforms like Twitter, Facebook, LinkedIn and Threads, summarizing the key insights and making it appealing for my target audience".*

***

# Your Guide To Customer Support

How about the customer service industry, then? How exactly should you navigate your job using the benefits that ChatGPT has to offer you?

## Step #1: Review the questions customers ask most frequently.

Working in the customer service industry, you're bound to find yourself answering the same kind of question from different customers. Say that you're on the customer service team of an app with a subscription. One of the most common questions you'll encounter will be, "How do I cancel my subscription?" or "How can I upgrade my account to premium?" or "I forgot my password." Now, you can spend hours and hours answering these same questions every day, or you can choose the sane option and have ChatGPT answer them, as I mentioned before. To do this, you'll have to identify what questions you're asked the most (Patterson, 2023).

## Step #2: Give ChatGPT the prompts it needs to generate answers.

Once you have identified the questions you're asked the most, you will need to provide ChatGPT with the prompt it needs to generate its answer. This way, when the app receives one of these questions, its response will be ready at hand, and the app's chatbot will be able to send it to the customer who asked it immediately and without bothering you once.

## Step #3: Have ChatGPT summarize long conversations.

As a customer service official, you may sometimes find yourself locked in long conversations with customers. This often happens, for instance, when a customer is experiencing a technical issue that you and your team are trying to solve. Odds are, you will recommend various solutions throughout your conversation, and the customer will try them out. If the conversation continues for long enough, you may start forgetting which solutions you've already asked them to try and which you haven't. That's perfectly normal since you're only human. Sure, you can scroll through your entire conversation history to check what you've said so far. However, this will cost you time, and you will risk skipping over something in the process.

A better strategy to follow in this case would be to ask ChatGPT to summarize the entire conversation, paying particular attention to what solutions have been tried thus far. This way, you can have a concise illustration of everything that has been done. You'll then be able to recommend a new solution to the customer. Alternatively, you can provide that summary to the tech team working on the glitch, thereby giving them a thorough understanding of what's wrong, what has been tried to fix it, and what they need to do next.

## Step #4: Categorize incoming questions.

As a general rule, the grand majority of the questions you receive will be very similar. As a customer service official, you'll seldom be asked a question that no other customer has ever asked before. That's a good thing, because you can use it to pick up speed and work more efficiently, so long as you categorize the different kinds of questions you receive.

Categorizing questions, or rather asking ChatGPT to categorize and label the questions you regularly receive, will help you in two ways. First, it'll allow you to spot frequently asked questions you might have missed. You'll then be able to use ChatGPT to generate answers for them. Second, it'll allow you to see any issues and problems quickly. By categorizing messages, you'll be able to notice that many different customers are having a specific type of technical issue with their app much more quickly than you otherwise could have. You'll therefore be able to alert the IT team to the issue much quicker and have it solved sooner.

## Step #5: Send notifications.

Replying to customer questions quickly is great, but what if you didn't have to? What if your customers could get the answers to their questions before they ever asked them? That might sound a little surreal, but it's actually very possible with ChatGPT. Say that there's a glitch on the app, and the IT team is working on it (Mottesi, 2023). You know that you will get a flood of messages from your customers asking you what's going on. A great strategy to employ here is to give ChatGPT a prompt telling it to write a message explaining what's going on and that the IT team will be resolving the matter shortly. Once the message is ready, you can have it sent out as a push notification. You can do the same once the technical issue has been resolved and let everyone know.

## Step #6: Reply to customer reviews.

Replying to customer reviews, be they positive or negative, is an old customer service trick, and it's a good one. In cases where you receive a bad review, this can help you to solve any problems your customer may be having and maybe even get them to change their review by helping them. In cases where the review is good, it adds a personal touch to things and makes customers feel special. However, replying to all your reviews can take a long time and prove really overwhelming, which is why you want to use ChatGPT for this. ChatGPT can craft personalized responses to different reviews and start conversations with customers.

## Step #7: Send special offers.

Often, brands, companies, and apps have special offers meant to appeal to and entice customers. Of course, customers need to be aware of these to be able to take advantage of them. Once more, you can painstakingly write down emails and notifications each time you have some news to share, and lose a lot of time and energy in the process. Alternatively, you can just have ChatGPT do this and spare yourself the hassle and the headache.

***

# Your Guide To Streamlining Business Processes

The thing about work is that it's always accompanied by these different tasks that seem to take up way too much of your time, no matter what industry you're in. These tasks are relatively minor but still important to do, so it's not like you can skip them. As you're doing them, you often think, "It'll just take me 5 minutes." Those minutes add up, however, costing hours if not days' worth of time in the long term. However, they don't have to. If you want, you can use ChatGPT to automate a number of these tasks and remove them from your plate, freeing up time which you can use for other, more productive things in the process:

## Step #1: Always automate mundane and repetitive work through automation.

The key to optimizing your business routine lies in simplifying mundane and repetitive work through automation. This is because such work can cost you an obscene amount of time. Things like managing your social media presence and bookkeeping fall into this category of work, and they're both things that ChatGPT can help get done faster. Once you've set up your OpenAI account, make a list of all these tedious tasks that you have to do regularly. This way, you will know exactly what to streamline and how to get started doing it (Severino, 2023).

## Step #2: Write down your operating procedures.

What if you're not sure which works you can streamline and which ones you can't? This is why you should write down your operating procedures. Every business has standard operating procedures. Writing these down with the help of ChatGPT will result in the creation of a step-by-step process. You will then be able to look at this process and identify precisely what you can automate and what you cannot.

## Step #3: Create an automated FAQ.

Creating an automated FAQ is a good idea because it's yet another way of quickly answering customers' questions about your brand, products, and services without them having to ask. It saves everyone a lot of time, energy, and effort, and improves everyone's experience as well (Trends, 2023).

## Step #4: Automate data analysis tasks.

Another kind of work that you should automate at the soonest opportunity is data analysis tasks (AIContentfy Team, 2023a). This includes things like arriving at various observations and insights by looking at large pools of data, collecting said data, and identifying patterns within them. All this is stuff that ChatGPT is a pro at, as you well know. By assigning these chores to it, you can gain the information you need to improve your products and services and meet your customers' needs in record time. As an extension of that, you'll be able to improve your marketing, customer service, and product development services.

## Step #5: Always streamline internal communication.

This one might not seem all that obvious, but it's a strategy that you'll come to appreciate and be really thankful for. Streamlining internal communication means automating messages and reminders, transcribing meetings, providing real-time translation during said meetings, and creating meeting summaries for all. Such things can ensure everyone is on the same page and keep misunderstandings and miscommunication to a minimum. This, in turn, will improve everyone's quality of work, as well as their ability to collaborate with one another.

## Step #6: Introduce ChatGPT to the HR department.

The HR department of a business might be the one department that has to do the most tedious, time-consuming work, like reading resume after resume. As such, this department would probably benefit most from ChatGPT's streamlining efforts. It would appreciate it the most, too. One thing ChatGPT can hasten up is the recruitment process. If you were to feed every resume that was sent to your company to ChatGPT, you'd be able to find the best fits for new positions quickly, send out emails inviting them in for interviews, schedule those interviews, and send out offers to the candidates of your choice without breaking a sweat. Beyond the recruitment process, you could create automated responses to frequently asked employee questions, manage employee records efficiently, evaluate employees' performance diligently and accurately, and even speed up the new employee onboarding process.

## Step #7: Start managing your inventory with ChatGPT.

This is a fairly obvious one when you think about it. If you are part of a business that deals with physical goods, then you need to keep careful track of those goods. Doing this with ChatGPT can both help you pick up speed and prevent anything from going missing or being misplaced thanks to regular old human error. ChatGPT can produce thorough records of your inventory, along with purchase orders. It can send those orders to suppliers, keep track of sales and turnover, and thus be able to help with demand planning and forecasts for the future.

# Key Takeaways

- To master ChatGPT, practice is essential, like perfecting culinary skills with a kitchen knife.

- ChatGPT is valuable in creating written content, from topic selection to outline creation and crafting meta-descriptions.

- It can help overcome writer's block and facilitate the creation of engaging social media posts.

- ChatGPT helps identify frequent customer questions and draft ready-made answers, saving time.

- Utilizing ChatGPT for crafting special offers and notifications enhances customer engagement.

- ChatGPT can automate repetitive work such as social media management and bookkeeping.

- You can use ChatGPT to automate messages, transcriptions, and translations during meetings.

- Integrating ChatGPT into the HR department can significantly speed up the recruitment process.

- Employing ChatGPT for inventory management helps in tracking goods and making demand forecasts, reducing human error.

- ChatGPT can facilitate data analysis, providing insights to improve products, services, and marketing strategies.

# Test Your Knowledge

As always, let's put what we have learned into practice. You're going to have to fire up ChatGPT and make use of it as part of this exercise:

You're a content creator that has been contracted by Ford to write an article about electric cars in an effort to promote their new ones. Your target demographic is Gen Z, and you want an article that's equal parts adventurous and eco-friendly. Create a prompt to generate 3 ideas for your article.

Your Prompt:

_____

_____

_____

_____

_____

The Ideas ChatGPT Has Given You:

1.

2.

3.

Choose one of these ideas or create a new prompt until you find an idea that you're satisfied with. Once you have, it'll be time to write your outline. Devise an outline prompt to give to ChatGPT:

_____

_____

_____

_____

_____

Once you have your outline, write or pretend to have written your article. All done? If that's the case, it's now time to write some prompts for your meta-descriptions:

_____

_____

_____

_____

_____

Your final step is to generate some social media posts. How about some prompts to get ChatGPT going?

    1.

    2.

    3.

Now that you've honed your skills through hands-on tutorials and exercises, let's explore how to troubleshoot and overcome common challenges while working with ChatGPT.

## Chapter Eight

# Smooth Sailing With ChatGPT—Tackling Troubles & Challenges

*"When you hit a wall, it's not the end of the road; it's a chance to grow stronger."*

Sarah Browne

There's this bizarre idea, nay, expectation, that almost all of us have that life is supposed to be easy and mostly obstacle-free. We operate under the illusion that we should never come across any hurdles, and as a result, we often give up way too quickly. We forget that challenges, obstacles, and hurdles are a part of life. This applies to every part and aspect of life, and that includes ChatGPT.

No matter how well you know this platform and how great you are at your chosen line of work, the fact of the matter is you're going to come across challenges occasionally. You'll encounter obstacles you need to overcome, glitches you need to fix, and issues you need to resolve. This is more than possible, so long as you can see the obstacles before you and know what to do to overcome them. For example, if you were a professional hurdler, you'd need to know how tall the hurdle you're facing mid-race is to leap over it. Furthermore, you'd need to know the exact technique you need to use to jump over that hurdle, and you'd need to practice it. Right here is where that practice begins.

## Identifying & Overcoming Obstacles

With that dramatic opening out of the way, what are the most common obstacles you can expect to encounter when using ChatGPT?

- **Accuracy**: While ChatGPT does work incredibly well, it doesn't and cannot know everything, as mentioned before, so sometimes it will generate incorrect answers. It even has the audacity to argue that the incorrect information it presents people with is correct. While it's expected that this flaw will be remedied as the bot becomes ever more developed, it's something that people using ChatGPT should be aware of. As a general rule, you should never believe 100% of everything you hear anyway, and this rule certainly applies here as well. This is doubly true with respect to the potential bias that comes with ChatGPT. ChatGPT can be biased in various ways, depending on what kind of information it has been trained on, as I explained in previous chapters.

- **Error 1020** means ChatGPT has detected something unusual in the network you're using and is blocking your access. Sometimes it shows up if you've visited the ChatGPT website one too many times in the day. One cheat to overcome this? Using a VPN like ExpressVPN, NordVPN, or CyberGhost can help you overcome this matter (Chavez, 2023).

- **Error 429** pops up when you've asked for too many things too quickly, like trying to buy 100 tickets when you're only allowed 10. It's there to make sure everyone gets a fair chance. If you run into this error, you'll just have to wait a little while before you can send another message. Also, if you haven't already, you might consider upgrading to ChatGPT-4. As you might recall, this upgrade allows you to unlock the full potential of ChatGPT; you won't run into this error as often and will receive even better responses. As a reminder, you have two pricing options: $0.03 per 1K prompt tokens or a monthly plan for $20 (which I think it's best!)

- **Login errors** usually occur either because you have expired cookies—not the edible kind but the virtual kind, which is a shame—in your browser or because you entered incorrect credentials. If you run into this issue, head to your browser's settings to clear out those old cookies, and that should clear the way for you to log in. If you're still having trouble and your login info is correct, using a VPN might help—especially if you're in a country that doesn't yet support ChatGPT.

- **Network errors** happen because your connection has timed out while you have been waiting for a response from ChatGPT.

- **"At capacity right now"** means that the server is super busy and can't take on any more tasks at the moment. It's like when a restaurant has every table filled, and you have to wait for a spot to open up. So just wait and after a while the problem should resolve itself on its own.

- **"Error in body stream"** means that the information sent to ChatGPT got jumbled or corrupted, like a letter getting smudged in the rain, and ChatGPT couldn't read it properly. This may be solved by checking and troubleshooting your internet connection.

Google "Ookla Speed Test" and then run said test on your internet connection. It may just be that your Wi-Fi has slowed down for whatever reason and is currently causing these issues. Try disconnecting and reconnecting to the Wi-Fi again, and resetting your network settings. Remember, the most basic rule in technological fixes is that turning on and turning off things usually fixes problems.

If the internet's fine, you might need to ask ChatGPT's support team for help. Just log in at the OpenAI website, scroll to the bottom, and click "Chat With Us" under the "Support" tab. Someone (or maybe even a bot) will answer quickly to help you out. (Chavez, 2023).

## General Troubleshooting

If the above fixes aren't resolving your issues or you're facing something else, don't worry! First, check if the issue is on ChatGPT's end by visiting downdetector.com or Status.OpenAI.com. If they show no problems, the service is working fine, and the issue lies elsewhere. Your next step could be to clear your browser cache, an easy fix that often works wonders.

Finally, you'd be surprised how often miscommunication between AI and humans can cause errors. Still, it's usually a simple fix, not a Terminator scenario. Simply slow down with your requests, rephrase your prompts and provide more context to ChatGPT.

## Key Takeaways

- Be aware of ChatGPT's accuracy and potential biases; they vary and are essential to understand.

- Overcome Error 1020 (detecting unusual activity) and 429 (too many requests) with patience or by using a VPN.

- Enhance your experience and reduce limitations by upgrading to ChatGPT-4.

- Fix login issues by clearing browser cookies or using a VPN.

- Solve the "Error in body stream" by troubleshooting your internet connection.

- Seek assistance from ChatGPT's support team, as they are readily available.

- Resolve misunderstandings in ChatGPT's responses by rephrasing prompts or providing more context.

# Test Your Knowledge

Now that you know the different kinds of errors you may experience and how to fix them, let's put your knowledge to the test.

**1. You tried accessing ChatGPT, but a login error suddenly appeared. You're pretty sure that your username and password are correct. What should you do?**

a) Double-check my internet connection and try logging in again

b) Contact customer support for assistance

c) Clear my browser cache and cookies before logging in again

**2. Which actions can help resolve "Error 429" related to exceeding the maximum number of ChatGPT requests allowed in a set amount of time?**

a) Refresh the webpage and try making the requests again

b) Implement a delay between consecutive requests to stay within the allowed limit

c) Contact support and request an increase in the request limit

**3. Which action(s) should you take when encountering an "Error in body stream"?**

a) Use a VPN

b) Contact customer support immediately

c) Troubleshoot my Wi-Fi connection

d) Log out and log back in

**4. What issues and errors can you solve with a VPN?**

a) Error 1020 (detecting unusual activity)

b) Signing in from an unauthorized country

c) Error 1020 and 429 (too many requests)

d) Error 1020 and signing in from an unauthorized country

**5. You've tried everything, but you can't seem to solve whatever issue you're having. It's time to reach out to the ChatGPT support team. How do you go about doing that?**

a) Log in to my ChatGPT Account, go to ChatGPT Playground, and ask for help

b) Log in to my OpenAI account, scroll to the bottom, and click "Chat With Us"

c) Go to my profile page and click on "Customer Support" in the lower left corner

Answers: 1-c, 2-b, 3-c, 4-d, 5-b

As we've explored the world of ChatGPT and learned how to troubleshoot common challenges, it's time to delve into the broader context of AI's transformative impact on industries and job roles. In the next chapter, we'll discuss the role of AI in shaping the future of work and the potential opportunities it presents.

## Chapter Nine

# AI Revolution—Transforming Industries & Shaping Job Roles

*"The only constant in life is change."*

Heraclitus

Recent developments in artificial intelligence have not only generated a lot of buzz but also given rise to a great deal of fear. The primary fear here is that AI and, mainly, ChatGPT will take people's jobs, as mentioned in the previous chapter. Is there any validity to this fear, though? AI and ChatGPT have certainly changed various industries, as we've seen, and it's undeniable that they've had an impact—and a rather large one at that—on the current job market. Is that impact a bad one, or does it have positive sides to it? The short answer is, *"Yes, of course it does."* The long answer entails looking at exactly how AI has changed the existing job market and, more importantly, how you can use those changes to your benefit.

## The Impact of AI On The Job Market

The idea that we're going to lose our jobs to AI isn't a new one. Truthfully, it's been around since AI was first conceived. It's probably just as old an idea that we will end up in some war with robots at some point in the future. Both make for really good stories and plot points, after all. However, that's all that they are. Stories. The truth of the matter is, while AI does and will impact the job market to some degree—it's inconceivable that it wouldn't—it's never going to replace us. At least, not in the way you'd think.

Think about it like this: Back before we had cell phones, everyone had home phones. You couldn't just call people up on those phones. You'd have to call the operator. An operator was one of many people sitting behind a desk plugging different cables into a massive device to connect phones so callers could talk to one another. Over time, phone technology changed. Suddenly, phones could call one another without needing an operator's services. Thus, operators became obsolete.

That doesn't mean, however, that former operators suddenly became jobless, at least not for the most part. Instead, they were trained for and moved into other positions in phone companies. A similar thing happened when computers were first introduced to NASA. Before computers, there used to be a team of women working in NASA calculating space flight trajectories by hand. When computers were first brought over to Nasa, it became clear that they would take these women's jobs. So, the women in question learned coding language. Thus, they could program the very computers that would "take" their jobs.

They were promptly given new jobs at NASA doing just that. This right here is precisely what will happen where AI is concerned as well. True, certain job descriptions may become obsolete thanks to AI. However, other, newer positions, jobs, and job descriptions will arise. People will then be trained for those jobs and start doing them instead.

As for what kinds of jobs AI will impact, the general consensus seems to be that in the not-so-distant future, jobs like manufacturing and ware-house positions will see a big shift, with inventories getting the automated treatment and everything moving around without a human touch. Then there's the world of research and data entry, where thanks to ChatGPT, stuff can be done super-fast, without much human intervention. Chatbots are already making waves in customer service, as you know. And if you're in insurance underwriting, ChatGPT could soon be drafting alongside you.

Certain industries, though, will be only minimally touched by AI. These industries require that "human touch," like teaching, for instance. For all the benefits that AI offers in education, which are many, as you saw, it can never take the place of a truly inspiring teacher. Neither can it ever replace lawyers, authors, poets, editors, medical professionals, therapists and mental health professionals, social workers, or management professionals (Thomas, 2019). The reason is simple: While AI is very good at doing certain things, it's not so great at others. It's not the best at using empathy, for instance, which a therapist or teacher (at least good ones) would absolutely need to do. It's not great at hand-eye coordination either, which AI can be forgiven for, I think, seeing as it doesn't usually come equipped with hands or eyes.

Aside from changing job descriptions and removing some positions from the board, AI will also change the workplace. This is evident in the amount of time AI allows you to free up in your day-to-day life by taking on those menial and repetitive tasks no one likes doing. That AI can take on such burdens is important because it increases your efficiency and productivity and improves your mental health, energy levels, and mood.

One of the most important contributions AI will make to the workforce and the workplace, though, is the creation of new jobs. This is bound to happen, as in the phone operators and NASA computers examples.

Just look at Netflix. They're on the lookout for someone who knows their way around AI to be part of their Machine Learning team (Matza, 2023). You might be thinking, *"Oh great, another big company is trying to switch out people for computers."* But here's something interesting: this team's main gig is working on that Netflix feature that suggests what you should watch next. And guess what? They're offering a whopping $900,000 a year for it, which has caught quite the attention in Hollywood.

Now, think beyond just Netflix. Imagine the additional roles that could emerge when we blend AI capabilities with human ingenuity. These aren't just roles for the tech-savvy but roles where humans leverage AI tools to enhance their own capabilities, and here's the kicker: A significant part of this job creation will result from the free time AI introduces into our routines.

This newfound time can be a treasure trove for innovation, brainstorming new projects, and taking initiatives in numerous areas. Furthermore, this surplus time becomes an opportunity for learning and training. As AI crafts new job profiles, it's only natural to acquire the skills for these roles. Companies can harness this 'extra' time, offering employees the required training. This symbiotic relationship ensures that not only do individuals retain their jobs and income, but companies also won't have to scout externally for talent, especially for these newly created positions.

Truthfully, these training efforts are already underway. Take Amazon, for instance. That Amazon has become increasingly automated as the years go by isn't news. This situation has created a lot of anxiety among its 300,000-strong workforce. The good news, however, is that Amazon has no intention of abandoning the employees that make up this workforce (Amazon Staff, 2023). Instead, it has started offering them a voluntary training known as Upskilling 2025, which essentially teaches employees, whose positions will eventually become fully automated, the technical skills they'll need for the next positions. Those employees can then take on jobs requiring those skills within Amazon and beyond it if they'd like.

You will have to adopt and cultivate certain specific skills in your training period, of course. Math skills, for instance, will be vital in the coming age of automation, as will creativity. The same can be said for verbal and written communication, emotional intelligence, problem-solving, critical thinking, and employee management skills.

As for which industries these new jobs will be created in, they're simply too many to count. Currently, experts agree that new jobs and positions will open up in all sorts of areas, including accounting, technical writing, forensic science, MRI operation, finance, web development and customer service, to name a few examples. Contrary to expectations, AI won't cause the existing job market to shrink. Instead, it'll allow it to grow, just as the Industrial Revolution did.

So, who should be most prepared to take on such training and prepare for new positions? Whose existing job descriptions will be changed because of AI's involvement with the workplace? Well, while AI will never replace doctors, artificial intelligence will become a part of their environment. It already is, thanks to the existence of things like predictive medicine (V. K, 2022). Given that, doctors and healthcare professionals must be prepared for AI interference in their day-to-day jobs, especially when making diagnoses, prescribing medicine, and keeping track of patient histories and records.

Customer service professionals are another group of people that can not only expect heavy AI interference but are already experiencing it. Currently, AI can take a lot off such professionals' plates, as we've seen, and the more advanced AI becomes, the more it will be able to take on too. What will probably end up happening, then, is that the customer service workforce will shrink. A small number of customer service officials will likely remain in the industry, tending to those customers whose problems can't be solved through AI interactions. The rest will have to be trained for other lines of work during this transitory period and thus, start taking on new responsibilities.

The financial sector, mainly banking and insurance, will see its fair share of AI interference too. AI is currently being used in fraud detection and to automate repetitive tasks in the field. Both these things free up bankers' and insurance officials' time. The same can be said for retail analysis. Once such analysis becomes fully automated, AI will be able to make accurate predictions for stock needs, as well as buying trends.

Meanwhile, self-checkout counters, like Amazon Go, will only increase in number. Even transportation is becoming entangled with AI, in the form of self-driving cars. This is bound to impact things like taxis and public transportation systems. Those drivers, conductors, and the like might have to be retrained as supervisors, monitoring all the self-driving vehicles, ensuring they operate in peak condition and keeping to their ascribed routes. Who knows, such things may even eventually tame that time-consuming beast known as traffic.

Going back to retraining for new, AI-created jobs, it's undeniable that these positions will require having certain AI skills. In fact, it's those very skills that most people being moved to new positions will be trained for (Verma, 2018). The essential skills that these new positions will be looking for among candidates will be:

- Problem-solving and critical thinking

- Deep learning

- Computing

- Robotics

- Machine learning

- Natural language processing (NLP)

- Data Science

These skills, in concert, give rise to the creation of a variety of different, new positions. In fact, positions like these are already emerging. For instance, machine learning engineers exist today. These engineers combine their software and NLP skills to work with data sets and craft modern software tools.

Modern data scientists are also running around, analyzing massive amounts of data using machine learning and making predictive analyses. On top of that, there are AI product managers who manage the creation and application of AI goods and services. There's something called an AI consultant too, who advises brands and companies on the best use of these products and services.

Deep learning engineers, meanwhile, create deep learning algorithms that address complex issues in fields such as healthcare and finance. As for the newest iteration of research assistants, they gather, analyze, and test out new algorithms with the help of AI, and even create new apps that use artificial intelligence.

These are just a few basic examples of all the new and exciting positions AI is giving birth to. Suffice it to say, then, that artificial intelligence is changing the workforce landscape, and those belonging to it will have to take it upon themselves to adapt.

## Adapting To An AI-Driven World

Luckily, we human beings are known for our adaptability. Hence, adapting to a new, AI-driven world will be a cinch, so long as you know what to expect. The training you'll have to undergo to achieve this is often referred to as *upskilling*. You've seen some of the new abilities you'll have to pick up as part of upskilling, like deep learning, NLP, and problem-solving. These, however, are not the only skills you may have to acquaint yourself with. There are bound to be other, newer, even unexpected ones, depending on how AI develops and progresses (*6 Upskilling Strategies in the World of AI*, 2023).

Suppose you want to adapt to the new landscape that AI is creating in the workplace. In that case, your first order of business is to identify precisely which skills are in demand. Do a quick search on Indeed, focusing on the new job descriptions popping up in your field. What are the people working in these fields looking for? What abilities are listed in those job descriptions, and how might you acquire them? What do you need to know to fulfill those job responsibilities?

Once you've identified what skills and knowledge you need, you will obviously have to learn them, seeing as you can't acquire new skills through osmosis alone (I wish!). Online learning is a great way to pick up the new skills you need. There are copious online resources available to you these days, be they video tutorials, Zoom lessons, or something else.

By participating in these courses, from the comfort of your own home, no less, you'll be able to expand your library of knowledge in no time. If you want to be a little more social, you can always attend industry events, such as conferences, panels, and seminars where these skills will be introduced to you. You'll also gain new insights about what you need to learn from other industry professionals by attending simple networking events.

Getting an apprenticeship of some sort or acquiring a mentor is one of the best ways of learning something, regardless of what industry you're in. Mentors are invaluable sources of guidance, wisdom, and knowledge. As such, finding one that's a good fit for you is very important. This is doubly true when you consider how mentors will usually be some of the first people to hear about new opportunities, developments, and job openings. They'll therefore be able to inform you of them well in advance, thus pushing you in the right direction and ensuring your advancement in your field.

Still, some of the skills you'll need to pick up to adapt to the changing workforce will be more on the technical side. They'll require dedicated work, which you can put in by going through professional training. Your workplace will typically offer such training to hire internally, and they're things you must take advantage of whenever possible. Only in doing so can you keep advancing your skills and growing your own toolkit of assets.

Judging from all this, one thing is quite clear: The key to adapting to an AI-driven world is continually pursuing knowledge and self-advancement. Lifelong learning is the only thing that can ensure you're never left behind in the work line you have chosen to be a part of.

## Future Trends & Growth Areas

Having said all that, there are some key areas where changes brought about by AI are bound to cause a veritable revolution. These areas are the purview of virtual assistants, design, and decision-making processes. The changes AI brings to virtual assistants' work and, by extension, customer service are immediately obvious. Just like chatbots are being widely used in the customer service industry to tend to customer needs, virtual assistants nowadays do a similar thing (Ishchenko, 2023).

Powered by ChatGPT, these assistants quickly and efficiently respond to their "employer's" queries, make reservations and schedule appointments, and even provide people with various recommendations of restaurants, stores, and more, like they were their own personal concierges. Over time these virtual assistants are expected to become even more advanced, so much so they might replace human assistants altogether. At the very least, they're bound to become a part of the lives of individuals who need two separate assistants to get through their workloads.

One emerging and fascinating trend in the world of virtual assistants is virtual reality. Should this technology ever become advanced enough, it's possible that your AI assistant will come with a virtual face and body of its own. Perhaps such virtual assistants will then be able to give visitors a tour of a company or walk them through the different goods and services the brand offers.

ChatGPT will significantly impact the realm of design too. Let's say you're an architect and must design a particular space. You'll be given specific parameters for this, like how large the building has to be, what materials are to be used—assume that the building is expected to be fully eco-friendly, for example—and whatnot. In such a case, you can enlist ChatGPT's help by giving it a prompt for the design. Said prompt will naturally include all the parameters you've been given to work with (Voltl, 2022). ChatGPT will then give you various explanations and ideas about how to go about creating your design. It can provide insight into what eco-friendly materials you can use for the building's insulation or how to create fire-resistant doors and walls.

Aside from that, ChatGPT will be able to give you an instantaneous but thorough understanding of the international building codes (IBC) you have to keep in mind when designing your buildings. This way, you can be sure that you're abiding by these codes without losing any valuable time or having to go back to adjust and fix things.

You can even use ChatGPT to develop documentation and productivity tools for 3D modeling. ChatGPT can do this by writing or debugging code that can create geometric areas for you to actively work with. You'll then be able to take those initial designs or outlines and develop them further, until you've achieved the architectural model you've been dreaming up.

In the same way, it shouldn't be at all surprising to hear that ChatGPT can significantly streamline both decision-making and communication processes within companies and among team members. The AI assistant that ChatGPT supplies people with can help a lot with the communication angle of things (*ChatGPT - Communication and Decision-Making*,

2023). That assistant can be incorporated into a lot of different messaging apps, for example, thereby helping to reduce miscommunication to a minimum and ensuring that everyone communicates with one another in a timely and thorough manner.

On the decision-making end of things, ChatGPT can streamline a lot of different processes by analyzing mountains of data quickly, and providing you with the information you need to make the right decisions going forward. This includes doing things like conducting market analysis and providing you with a list of changes you need to get on board with to stay current in the industry as it exists and will come to exist in the near future.

# Key Takeaways

- Upskilling is indispensable for navigating an AI-influenced job landscape.

- Job market research ensures awareness of AI-driven shifts in industry demands.

- Leveraging online learning platforms is essential for acquiring AI-related skills.

- Networking and industry events are crucial for firsthand knowledge of AI trends.

- Mentorships offer insights and opportunities in an AI-transforming workforce.

- Internal workplace training is a golden opportunity for skill enhancement.

- Commitment to lifelong learning is the backbone of staying relevant amidst AI advancements.

- AI's influence on virtual assistants is transforming customer and personal assistance dynamics.

- ChatGPT is becoming instrumental in design, modeling, and construction processes.

- AI enhances decision-making efficiency by rapidly processing and analyzing vast data sets.

## Reflection Prompts

As you can see, ChatGPT has influenced and will continue to influence the existing workforce significantly. When you lay out all the changes at once, it's kind of a "wow" moment, right? And let's be real; when these shifts are happening day by day, they can sneak right by us. Given all that, it's wise to think about what might be shifting in your own field right now. So, take a moment and think about your industry. How has AI shaken things up in the last 10 years? What about the past 5, or even just this last year? When you've got a clear picture, jot down everything you've noticed. Next up, think about where all this might be headed and what new skills you might need to learn to stay ahead of the curve.

_____

_____

_____

_____

_____

_____

_____

We're nearing the end, yet a vital piece of the puzzle is left to explore. Like a hammer that can either build or destroy, AI is a potent tool, and its results depend on how you use it. Next, we'll delve into the world of AI ethics and the safe use of ChatGPT. While this is the final stretch, it is perhaps the most important one. If it sounds boring, do not worry. I'm keeping it short!

## Chapter Ten

# Ensuring A Bright AI Future In The Ethical Landscape of AI

*"With great power comes great responsibility."*

Spider-Man / Uncle Ben

A s valuable as AI clearly is to us human beings, it must be noted that there are certain valid concerns surrounding it. These concerns essentially have to do with privacy and security, ethical use of technology, and bias. The thing about technology is that it's never inherently bad or good. It all depends on who's using it and for what purposes. So, what does using AI responsibly really mean? Let's see...

## Privacy & Security Concerns

Imagine this scenario: AI, as we've discussed, handles enormous volumes of data. More often than not, this data is "personal" - it relates directly to the individual human beings that are your customers. Picture yourself as a business owner deploying AI, such as ChatGPT. Suppose your objective is to build a responsible brand that maintains the trust and loyalty of its customers. In that case, robust data protection is non-negotiable. This implies a commitment to preventing personal information like health or financial records from falling into the wrong hands or being jeopardized by viruses and hacking attempts. Additionally, it means you must remain alert to potential computer fraud (Soo, n.d.).

You can do several things to keep your guard against such threats. The first is to be vigilant against and aware of browser extensions and fake AI apps. When downloaded, such extensions and apps can cause you to get hacked or become infected with a nasty virus that either damages or steals your valuable data. If you're considering downloading a specific app or extension, you must always do your research thoroughly and well, and only download it after you've been able to verify its effectiveness and validity. If you have any doubts about that app or extension, then obviously, you must forgo it (7 Essential Cyber Security Tips When Using ChatGPT and AI Tools, 2023).

One security measure to protect your data is clearing your ChatGPT chat history of all company and people names (even yours) before downloading an AI tool. This way, you can ensure the data is safe, even if said tool proves malicious.

Another precaution is to refrain from entering sensitive information into ChatGPT while using AI tools. Data that's not in a system cannot be stolen or corrupted, after all.

Additionally, if you're a developer, one added security measure you must take is thoroughly reviewing all AI-generated codes before you even think about using them. This way, you can spot potential problems and issues by using your expertise before they cause you a headache.

## Ethical Use Of AI Technology

What does it mean to use AI technology ethically? Simply put, it means pursuing a policy of accountability, confidentiality, and transparency concerning other people's data (Kenthapadi, 2019). It further means valuing fairness, which means making unbiased decisions when using ChatGPT and other AI devices.

Fairness goes hand in hand with accountability, since that means identifying and taking responsibility for a decision that your AI executes, including any biased choices that may have been made. While this might be hard to do, it's vital. Especially if, like in our example, you're a business owner. It is essential if you don't want to lose your customers' trust and if you want to correct whatever mistakes were made, which you should want to do.

Meanwhile, confidentiality plainly refers to keeping your customers' private information and data safe and secure. I mean, no one will want to work with your brand if they know their medical or credit card information will be leaked. No one will want to work with you either if it comes to light that you're in the habit of selling people's private information to marketing companies and the like without their permission and knowledge. These privacy and safety concerns extend to those who use ChatGPT for personal reasons, too. After all, even if you're just using it for fun, you're not sharing any less data and information with ChatGPT than others are. Hence, it's understandable that you'd be concerned with your private information suddenly being shared with a horde of strangers.

Finally, there's transparency, which is exactly what it sounds like: being transparent in everything, without hiding anything. Again, this goes along well with confidentiality and even accountability. It also fits in well with explainability, which is your ability to thoroughly and clearly explain why you made a decision or took a specific action. All of these things are liable to increase the trust and faith people place in you, thereby ensuring their brand loyalty and drawing even more potential customers your way. As a general rule in life and business, your reputation is something that can either make or break you. Obviously, you want the kind of reputation that can catapult you to the forefront of your industry, which is what ethical use of AI is all about.

## Understanding AI Bias

The final thing you need to be mindful of when using AI is bias. Just like a person can have biases based on their experiences, ChatGPT can also develop biases based on the information it was trained on, as we discussed earlier in the book. So, when you're training ChatGPT, think about it like teaching a child - you must be careful about what you feed it (Dilmegani, 2020).

ChatGPT can end up with two kinds of biases: the ones that sneak in without you noticing (cognitive biases) and those that pop up when it doesn't have enough diverse information to learn from. If, for example, you train ChatGPT on romance novels exclusively written by men and then expect it to write a romance short story, readers may later notice that the story is a little too male-gaze-y for their tastes. How could that not be the case when you haven't given ChatGPT a single example of a work written by a woman?

So, how do you make sure your AI isn't falling into these bias traps?

Start by looking at the information you're feeding ChatGPT. Is it diverse and comprehensive? If not, try adding more varied data. To help with this, you can do something called a subpopulation analysis. It's like checking how well your AI is doing with different groups of data. A hidden bias might need fixing if it's not doing equally well across the board.

In addition to that, you can also adopt a debiasing strategy, which comes in three flavors: technical, organizational, and operational.

The technical part is about using tools to spot and weed out potential biases, kind of like using a metal detector to find hidden treasures. The organizational part is about being transparent about how you're dealing with biases within your company. The operational part is all about making your data collection more diverse and complete.

All of this can seem a bit overwhelming, but don't worry! If you ever get to this point of complexity - there are tools out there that can make this easier. One of these is called AI Fairness 360, an open-source tool that's like a detective for finding and fixing biases. You can also use Google's What-If tool, which tests hypothetical situations to see how fair or unfair your AI is.

As long as you try to watch out for and tackle these biases, you will be in good shape to ensure your ChatGPT is as fair and balanced as possible.

# Key Takeaways:

- Robust data protection is essential for maintaining customer trust in AI applications.

- Be vigilant against fake AI apps and browser extensions to secure your data.

- Clear ChatGPT chat history of sensitive information as a precaution.

- Developers should review AI-generated codes for potential security risks.

- Ethical AI use involves accountability, confidentiality, and transparency.

- Address biases in AI systems to ensure fairness and ethical operation.

- AI bias can arise from the data it was trained on; diversity in data is key.

- Utilize debiasing strategies across technical, organizational, and operational levels.

- Tools like AI Fairness 360 help identify and mitigate biases in AI systems.

Now, having nailed down the ethical side of AI, we're ready to explore new territories. Stick around for the next chapter as we dig into the wider AI world, discover how ChatGPT interacts with other nifty tools, and daydream about the future of AI and language models.

## Chapter Eleven

# Venturing Beyond ChatGPT & Into The AI Ecosystem

*"The pace of progress in artificial intelligence (I'm not refer-ring to narrow AI) is incredibly fast. Unless you have direct ex-posure to groups like Deepmind, you have no idea how fast—it is growing at a pace close to exponential. The risk of something seriously dangerous happening is in the 5-year timeframe. Ten years at most."*

Elon Musk

As massively useful as ChatGPT is, it is still just one single tool making up the current AI landscape. There are many more. There are so many, in fact, that it's a little hard to believe. Some of these tools can be used as alternatives to ChatGPT. Others can be integrated with it. If you want to understand what you truly can achieve with ChatGPT, you must develop a comprehensive understanding of these alternatives and the overall landscape that they are a part of.

## Other AI-Driven Tools and Platforms

While you can use many ChatGPT alternatives, the best among them are:

- **Bard** is an AI tool developed by Google, because in what alternate universe wouldn't Google build its own AI chatbot? Like Chat-GPT, Bard uses machine learning and NLP to create real-time responses to your prompts (Gwira, 2023). It's user-friendly, replete with an array of interesting features, and can do many nifty things like translating between languages. It also has a "Google It" feature, along with Google Assistant and Alexa integration.

- **JasperAI**, on the other hand, is an excellent software writing program that meets various individuals', businesses', and brands' needs. It can quickly create SEO-friendly content, which is why it's favored among content creators and marketing strategists. What makes it unique, however, is its generative AI platform, where users can generate content that's tailor-made for their needs without having to input all the information needed manually.

- **ChatSonic** may be the best ChatGPT alternative currently available to the masses as an AI-powered writing tool and chatbot. Aside from being a phenomenal writing tool, you can use it to create digital works of art, too. Some of the best things about it are that you can give it voice commands to execute the tasks you want, and it can easily switch between languages.

- **CoPilot** is a final ChatGPT alternative to consider, and is best at writing code. As such, it's thought of very highly among developers. It can analyze code, give users real-time suggestions, and predict how developers can write code much faster than human users. It can autocomplete different kinds of code as well, and is, therefore, a great fit for both those new to coding and pros at it.

To stay updated on my exploration of these AI tools and have exclusive access to more awesome books coming up, I invite you to sign up for my newsletter so I can let you know whenever I uncover new insights. To do this, go to: https://brechtdinardo.com/

## Integrating ChatGPT Into Other Tools

As for which other tools ChatGPT can be integrated with, once more, there are many options. Some examples of different apps and tools that you can connect to your chatbot are:

- **Click Me Up**, which is great for project management

- **Microsoft Excel**, which by now is every business professional's favorite (or most hated) friend

- **Facebook Messenger**, which doesn't need all that much explaining, really

- **Spotify**, because who doesn't want to listen to music while working?

- **Many Chat**, which is often used for social media marketing purposes

If you want to integrate one or more tools like the ones mentioned here to your ChatGPT, then you'll have to navigate your way to the Chatbot settings tab in your OpenAI account (How to Embed ChatGPT in Your Website, 2023). Here, you'll name your bot, choose your avatar, then select your chatbot type, which will be "ChatGPT with Open AI." After that, you'll have to choose your chat model—for example, GPT-3.5—and copy your OpenAI API Key into text space before you. You'll then be able to customize your bot by integrating whatever tool you want into it. Simple as that! Many YouTube videos can show you these things step-by-step if you're more of a visual learner.

Now, to finalize our journey, let's dive into a treasure trove of additional resources and tools designed to enhance your ChatGPT experience and productivity.

## Chapter Twelve

# ChatGPT's Treasure Trove Of Resources & Tools

*"The reason why ChatGPT is so exciting is it's the exact right form factor for demonstrating how AI could become a useful assistant for nearly every type of work. We've gone from the theoretical to practical overnight."*

Aaron Levie

There's an old saying: There's never any end to learning. In no field is this truer than in the field of artificial intelligence, especially considering how rapidly it has evolved and still is evolving. What this means is that there's still so much that you can learn about both AI and ChatGPT. While this book is an excellent start for your ChatGPT journey, there's a lot more for you to discover. With that in mind, here's a comprehensive list of all the tools and resources you can use to discover all of ChatGPT's intricacies.

## Online Forums & Communities

- **ChatGPT Society:** If you made it this far, you deserve to be part of our private Facebook group, the go-to community to dive deeper into the thrilling world of AI & ChatGPT. You can connect with me and other fellow enthusiasts there, gain exclusive access to resources and learn from each other. Join us here: www.facebook.com/groups/chatgptsociety/

- **OpenAI API Forum:** A valuable platform that offers informative discussions about ChatGPT directly from the developers' perspective. Find it here: https://community.openai.com

- **Artificial Intelligence Stack Exchange:** This platform is an efficient source for broadening your AI knowledge. It provides comprehensive insights into different AI concepts such as neural networks, deep learning, and reinforcement learning. While it doesn't offer the same community feel as our Facebook group, it's still a robust resource, and you can check it out here: https://ai.stackexchange.com/

## Recommended Courses & Tutorials

If you learn best by watching videos, taking notes, and reading course materials, here is a current list of the best courses and tutorials for you to take:

- IBM Applied AI

- MLOPS

- AI for Everyone

- AI for Business—University of Pennsylvania

- IBM AI Engineering

- Prompt Engineering for ChatGPT—Vanderbilt University

- AI Product Management—Duke University

- OpenAI API Introduction

## Additional Software & Tools

There are other, additional tools you could explore as well. If you feel like doing so, the best ones to take advantage of are (Zhou, 2023):

- **Melany**, which allows you to use AI as your personal trainer

- **ChatGPT for Google**, which is the Chrome extension you didn't know you needed

- **Talk-to-GPT**, which is a voice-to-text system that makes Chat-GPT a whole lot more accessible to many

- **ChatGPT in WhatsApp**, which (as you might have guessed) integrates the AI into WhatsApp

Now that you've got all these fantastic resources and tools at your fingertips, what's next? How do you make sure you're really getting the most out of your ChatGPT experience? Well, it's time to get a bit more personal and reflective. Let's dive into something that will help you track your progress, struggles, and wins.

# Your ChatGPT Diary

The best way to see your progress, figure out how to get better, and find some inspiration is to keep a ChatGPT diary. If you're unsure as to how to start one, here's a handy template that can get you going:

**Date:** _____

**Goals:**

_____

_____

_____

_____

_____

**What did I discover today?**

_____

_____

_____

_____

_____

**What did I struggle with?**

_____

_____

_____

_____

_____

**What did I learn?**

_____

_____

_____

_____

_____

**What did I achieve?**

_____

_____

_____

_____

_____

**What do I want to learn?**

_____

_____

_____

_____

_____

**What do I want to achieve?**

_____

_____

_____

_____

_____

Alright, with those insights tucked under our belt,  let's turn the page and give this journey the perfect finish. Shall we?

# Conclusion

I n our world where fun distractions often take the front seat, I truly appreciate you sticking with me on this educational ride. We've delved into how ChatGPT can bring real value to your life or business, transforming it from a mystical tech entity to an everyday assistant that can simplify your life and help you be more efficient.

Yes, ChatGPT will stir significant changes in various sectors; that's a given. But with these changes, equal amounts of opportunities will be born—opportunities that you are perfectly positioned to seize, provided you keep an open mind toward this groundbreaking technology.

My utmost wish is that this book has equipped you with the knowledge and confidence to embrace these changes. In this spirit, remember, you're never sailing these waters alone. A community of fellow explorers, brought together by a shared enthusiasm for AI, is waiting to welcome you on Facebook. Please join us there to keep learning and to share your wins, challenges, and any questions you might have. We'll be thrilled to welcome you. Just follow this link: https://facebook.com/groups/chatgptsociety

To wrap it up, as someone wisely put it: *"Helping one person might not change the world, but it could change the world for that one person."* If this sentiment resonates with you, take a moment to share your feedback about this book on Amazon. Your insight could be the guiding star for someone still hesitant, helping them realize how ChatGPT can be a life-changing asset. To leave a review, find the book on Amazon and click on *"Write a customer review"* towards the bottom of the page, or simply scan the QR code below:

Thank you once more for your steadfast commitment. I'm excited to see where this shared journey with ChatGPT takes us next!

# Bonus Content

This is the part you'll want to dive into if you're interested in going beyond the basics and exploring more advanced features. Here, we delve into the intricacies of setting up your API key and maximizing your ChatGPT experience.

## Setting Up Your API Key

As you no doubt have figured out by now, how you use your ChatGPT account is entirely up to you and the possibilities are nearly endless. Before you can start playing around in your ChatGPT account, you'll need to choose your API Key (Marks, 2023). I can almost hear you asking what that is. The acronym "API" stands for Application Process Interface. Essentially, it is the mechanism that enables the different software components of ChatGPT to converse and work with one another. Put another way, it is a kind of technology that makes it very easy for you to converse with your AI. An API key, on the other hand, is a unique identifier you use to activate or unlock a specific API (*What Is an API Key?*, n.d.)

Now, as for how to choose your API key... The first thing you need to do is log in to your OpenAI account. Once you do, you'll encounter a "View API Key" button and here, you'll be able to select the ChatGPT API Key. The ChatGPT API Key was launched in March of 2023, and it is something you need if you want to be able to use the ChatGPT API, it makes it very easy for you to integrate GPT's various capabilities into different platforms and applications, making your life—and work—a great deal easier in the process.

So, you have clicked on the "View API Keys" icon, which can be found on the top-right corner of the webpage. Next, you'll need to click on the "Create an API Key" icon, which will allow you to set yours up. Don't worry, you won't have to do any coding or anything like that. Instead, the system will generate your key for you and you'll just have to copy-paste it in the area that reads "API Key" on the "OpenAI API" page. With those steps out of the way, you'll be able to use your key. To do that, you'll need to click on "View API Keys" again, where, this time, you'll need to choose your language preferences—you don't have to go with English if you don't want to—as well as your programming preferences. You can choose JavaScript over Python, as a most basic example. Then, you'll need to download either the library you have chosen for that language or the right SDK—software development kit—for it.

With that done, you'll finally be able to use your API key to generate a new instance of your API and start making requests of ChatGPT by giving it prompts. Your ChatGPT will respond to these prompts in mere seconds, thus saving you oodles of time.

It must be noted, of course, that while the basic version of ChatGPT is free, the ChatGPT API Key isn't, and neither is the premium version of the program. The good news is, when you first create your account, you'll be given $18 of free credit, which you'll be able to find on the API Keys page.

Once your free credit is done, however, you will start having to pay to use your key, which luckily isn't expensive by any definition of the word. Currently, 1000 tokens—meaning around 750 words—equals $0.002, which is more than reasonable if you think about it.

# The Benefits Of ChatGPT Playground

We've mentioned ChatGPT Playground a couple of times throughout this book. So what exactly is it? The Playground is basically a great way to familiarize yourself with ChatGPT (Reji, 2023). This was the very purpose for which ChatGPT-3 Playground was created. To use ChatGPT-3 Playground, you'll first have to sign into your OpenAI account, then click on "Playground," which'll be located at the top-right corner of the page. Here, you'll find a large text area for you to write prompts in and a settings bar to the right of the page. The settings will be made up of the following parameters: Model, Temperature, Maximum Length, Stop Sequences, Top P, Frequency Penalty, Best Of, Inject Start Test, Inject Restart Test.

What do all these mean and what are they for? Well, "Models" are the systems used to break down large texts into tokens, so that they can be understood by the system. If your text includes a big word like "evanescence" for example, that word will be broken down to its syllables, more or less. If it includes short words, however, like "dog" or "hot," then those will be taken as they are, without being broken down. The Playground has four key models: Ada, Babbage, Curie, and DaVinci. Before you ask, yes, they have all been named after famous scientists. Of these, DaVinci is considered to be the most capable since it performs incredibly well. This is why it is also the most costly model. Ada, on the other hand, is the least costly and fastest model to choose.

There's a button near the top of the page, above the big text box that reads "Load a Preset." This is useful for choosing a preset menu, so that you don't have to bother adjusting all these different parameters you are unfamiliar with. When you click on this button, a dropdown menu will appear and you'll be able to choose from options like "Chat," "Q&A," and "English to Other Languages." The system will then adjust the parameters to the side of the screen according to the preset mode you have chosen. Simultaneously, text will appear in the text box written in the format you have gone with. You'll now be able to replace the text with whatever it is you'd like to write, without losing the format in question.

That being said, you'll still be able to tweak the features that are to the side. One such feature is "Temperature," which allows you to fine tune the responses ChatGPT generates for you. If the temperature is close to zero, then the responses you'll be given will be more random. If, on the other hand, you raise the temperature, you'll make the response text a great deal more detailed and concrete. At the same time, you'll be able to adjust things like the length of the text, so that it is exactly as long or short as you need it to be.

The Playground essentially allows you to play around with all these different features and see what they can do firsthand. This experience comes in very handy when you go to your ChatGPT page and start using it for work or school. So, it is important that you explore it, especially when you first create your account. At that point, you'll be able to use your $18 credit to play around in the playground. Once that credit is up, however, you'll need to pay $0.06 for every 4,000 characters the Playground generates.

Whether you're planning on using ChatGPT for work, school, or personal endeavors, mastering these additional features will undoubtedly elevate your experience. Again, a heartfelt thank you for journeying to the end of this book. If you have any further questions, join our Facebook group—I'll see you there!

# References

Abby. (2023, March 20). Build a customer service bot with ChatGPT and extract information. Help Landbot. https://help.landbot.io/article/ulyso4n86h-build-a-customer-service-bot-with-chat-gpt-and-extract-information

Abdulrahman, S. (2023, March 14). Journalism meets AI: How chat GPT can revolutionize your work process and content creation. LinkedIn. https://www.linkedin.com/pulse/journalism-meets-ai-how-chat-gpt-can-revolutionize-your-abdulrahman/

AIContentfy Team. (2023a, January 23). ChatGPT and business: Streamlining operations. AIContentfy. https://aicontentfy.com/en/blog/chatgpt-and-business-streamlining-operations

AIContentfy Team. (2023b, March 5). ChatGPT and the entertainment industry: Transforming storytelling. AIContentfy. https://aicontentfy.com/en/blog/chatgpt-and-entertainment-industry-transforming-storytelling-1

Artificial Intelligence Stack Exchange. (n.d.). Artificial Intelligence Stack Exchange. https://ai.stackexchange.com/

Avasthi, A. (2021, October 5). The evolution of NLP. Datasaur.ai. https://datasaur.ai/blog-posts/the-evolution-of-nlp#:~:text=NLP%20is%20constantly%20evolving%20and

Bachini, J. (2023, January 16). Advanced ChatGPT prompt engineering. James Bachini. https://jamesbachini.com/advanced-chatgpt-prompt-engineering/

Browne, S. (2019, July 24). 17 things to remember when you hit the wall in life. Lifehack. https://www.lifehack.org/840652/hit-the-wall-in-life

ChatGPT - Communication and decision-making. (2023, March 27). Intrafocus. https://www.intrafocus.com/2023/03/chatgpt-communication-and-decision-making/

ChatGPT for customer service: Capabilities, use cases, and limitations. (n.d.). Thankful AI. https://www.thankful.ai/chatgpt-for-customer-service

ChatGPT integrations. (n.d.). Zapier. https://zapier.com/apps/chatgpt/integrations

Chatgpt quotes (29 quotes). (n.d.). GoodReads. Retrieved May 20, 2023, from https://www.goodreads.com/quotes/tag/chatgpt

ChatGPT: What to know about this AI content writing tool. (n.d.). Mailchimp. Retrieved May 26, 2023, from https://mailchimp.com/resources/chat-gpt-ai-content-writing/

Chatman, S. (2023, March 18). Creating engaging content with ChatGPT and notepad. LinkedIn. https://www.linkedin.com/pulse/creating-engaging-content-chatgpt-notepad-sean-chatman-/

Chavez, D. (2023, March 25). Top 10 common ChatGPT errors and fixes. UPDF. https://updf.com/knowledge/chatgpt-errors-and-fixes/

Chowdhury, M. (2021, August 11). The evolution of artificial intelligence: Past, present & future. Analytics Insight. https://www.analyticsinsight.net/the-evolution-of-artificial-intelligence-past-present-future/

Cloudbooklet Team. (2023, May 10). All you need to know about ChatGPT Playground. Cloudbooklet. https://www.cloudbooklet.com/chat-gpt-playground/

Cretu, C. (2023, April 6). How does ChatGPT actually work? An ML engineer explains. Scalable Path. https://www.scalablepath.com/data-science/chatgpt-architecture-explained

Diaz, M. (2023, April 13). How to use ChatGPT: Everything you need to know. ZDNET. https://www.zdnet.com/article/how-to-use-chatgpt/

Dilmegani, C. (2020, September 12). Bias in AI: What it is, types & examples, how & tools to fix it. AppliedAI. https://research.aimultiple.com/ai-bias/

Dilmegani, C. (2023, March 11). 7 ChatGPT coding use cases in 2023. AI Multiple. https://research.aimultiple.com/chatgpt-coding/

Dreamanart Team. (2023, March 12). ChatGPT: The revolutionary LInguage model transforming writing, education, psychology, and beyond. LinkedIn. https://www.linkedin.com/pulse/chatgpt-revolutionary-language-model-transforming-writing-education/

El Atillah, I. (2023, March 15). OpenAI's GPT-4 is here - and it's smarter than ever. Euronews. https://www.euronews.com/next/2023/03/15/gpt-4-openai-has-released-a-new-version-of-its-chatgpt-chatbot-but-whats-different

Gonzales, L. (2023, January). Elevate your ChatGPT game: Crafting an effective priming prompt. LinkedIn. https://www.linkedin.com/pulse/elevate-your-chatgpt-game-crafting-effective-priming-prompt-gonzales/?trk=pulse-article_more-articles_related-content-card

Govender, S. (2023, February 16). 120+ AI statistics: How the game is changing in 2023. MarketSplash. https://marketsplash.com/ai-statistics/

Great Learning Staff. (2023, March 20). ChatGPT for data analysts. Great Learning Blog: Free Resources What Matters to Shape Your Career! https://www.mygreatlearning.com/blog/chatgpt-for-data-analysts/

Gwira, C. (2023, April 16). 8 Best ChatGPT alternatives in 2023 (free and paid). Elegant Themes Blog. https://www.elegantthemes.com/blog/business/best-chatgpt-alternatives#3-bard

Harris, L. (2020, November 11). Text tokens. Steinberg.help. https://steinberg.help/dorico/v3/en/dorico/topics/engrave_mode/engrave_mode_frames_text_tokens_r.html#:~:text=Text%20tokens%20are%20codes%20that

How to embed ChatGPT in your website. (2023, May 16). Social Intents Knowledge Base. https://help.socialintents.com/article/189-how-to-embed-chatgpt-in-your-website#:~:text=Add%20your%20OpenAI%20API%20Key%20to%20Social%20Intents&text=Click%20on%20the%20Chatbot%20Settings

Introducing ChatGPT Plus. (2023, February 1). OpenAI. https://openai.com/blog/chatgpt-plus

Ishchenko, V. (2023, March 7). Revolutionizing customer service with ChatGPT: The future of personalized assistance. LinkedIn. https://www.linkedin.com/pulse/revolutionizing-customer-service-chatgpt-future-viktor-ishchenko/

Kenthapadi, K. (2019, May 11). Fairness, accountability, confidentiality, and transparency in AI/ML systems. LinkedIn. https://www.linkedin.com/pulse/fairness-accountability-confidentiality-transparency-aiml-kenthapadi/

Kesherim, R. (2023, March 29). 50+ healthcare industry statistics, facts & trends. Supportive Care ABA. https://www.supportivecareaba.com/statistics/healthcare-industry#:~:text=The%20healthcare%20industry%20is%20one

Kidd, S. (2023, March 13). How to use ChatGPT to simplify your content creation. Laire Digital. https://www.lairedigital.com/blog/chatgpt-vs-original-content/

Kochovski, A. (2023, March 24). ChatGPT statistics, facts & trends 2023 [How it works & its uses]. Cloudwards. https://www.cloudwards.net/chatgpt-statistics/

León, P. (2023, January 12). How to use ChatGPT & the benefits (complete guide 2023). Mind Designs. https://mindesigns.com.au/blog/how-to-use-chatgpt/#pp-toc__heading-anchor-1

Lynch, S. (2017). Andrew Ng: Why AI is the new electricity. Stanford Graduate School of Business. https://www.gsb.stanford.edu/insights/andrew-ng-why-ai-new-electricity

Mark. (2023, April 22). How to get ChatGPT API key free & use it. MLYearning. https://www.mlyearning.org/chat-gpt-api-key/

Marr, B. (2023, March 3). The top 10 limitations of ChatGPT. Forbes. https://www.forbes.com/sites/bernardmarr/2023/03/03/the-top-10-limitations-of-chatgpt/?sh=46a6ddf78f35

Miley. (2023, March 26). [Complete guide] ChatGPT login: How to create an account, log in, and troubleshoot. Awesome Screenshot. https://www.awesomescreenshot.com/blog/knowledge/chatgpt-login

Mok, A. (2023, March 26). What Elon Musk, Bill Gates, and 12 other business leaders think about AI tools like ChatGPT. Business Insider. https://www.businessinsider.com/elon-musk-bill-gates-business-leaders-quotes-on-chatgpt-ai-2023-2#bill-gates-american-business-magnate-and-cofounder-of-microsoft-1

Moore, S. (2023, March 27). What does ChatGPT mean for Healthcare? News-Medical.net. https://www.news-medical.net/health/What-does-ChatGPT-mean-for-Healthcare.aspx

Mottesi, C. (2023, February 8). 6 Uses of ChatGPT for customer service. Blog.invgate.com. https://blog.invgate.com/chatgpt-for-customer-service

Nguyen, H. (2023, March 23). How to make quizzes in just 10 minutes using ActivePresenter and ChatGPT? Atomi Systems,

Inc. https://atomisystems.com/elearning/make-quizzes-in-10-minutes-using-activepresenter-and-chatgpt/

Ogulcan. (n.d.). ChatGPT for studying: Best prompts & ways to use. StudySmarter UK. https://www.studysmarter.co.uk/magazine/chatgpt-for-studying/

Ohiri, M. (2023, March 8). Will ChatGPT displace traditional learning? Analyzing the potential of chatbots education. EducateMe. https://www.educate-me.co/blog/chatbots-in-education#:~:text=Personalized%20learning%3A%20One%20of%20the

OpenAI developer forum. (n.d.). OpenAI Developer Forum. https://community.openai.com/

Paruchuri, V. (2023, March 20). How does ChatGPT work? Dataquest. https://www.dataquest.io/blog/how-does-chatgpt-work/#:~:text=Tokens%20are%20fragments%20of%20text

Patterson, M. (2023, May 18). Using ChatGPT for customer service. Help Scout. https://www.helpscout.com/blog/chatgpt-customer-service/

Pietschmann, C. (2023, February 24). Crafting effective AI prompts for improved content generation: A ChatGPT guide. Build5Nines. https://build5nines.com/crafting-effective-ai-prompts-for-improved-content-generation-a-chatgpt-guide/

Pine, O. (2023, January 23). How automation can lead to the creation of new jobs . G7 Tech Services. https://g7techservices.com/news/how-automation-can-lead-to-the-creation-of-new-jobs/#:~:text=Another%20way%20automation%20can%20lead

Reji, A. R. (2023, February 15). Exploring the GPT-3 Playground- A beginner's guide. The Sec Master. https://thesecmaster.com/exploring-the-gpt-3-playground-a-beginners-guide/#What_is_GPT-3_Playground

Rule-based vs. statistical vs. neural machine translation. (2021, August 25). Summa Linguae. https://summalinguae.com/language-technology/rule-based-machine-translation-vs-statistical-and-neural-machine-translation/

Sacolick, I. (2023, February 27). ChatGPT and software development. InfoWorld. https://www.infoworld.com/article/3689172/chatgpt-and-software-development.html

Saeed, A. (2023, January 25). Best uses of ChatGPT for entertainment you never knew in 2023. Medium. https://bootcamp.uxdesign.cc/best-uses-of-chatgpt-for-entertainment-you-never-knew-in-2023-76dab4f2e3ea?gi=47daf013498c

Saltz, J. (2023, March 30). ChatGPT and data science projects. Data Science Process Alliance. https://www.datascience-pm.com/chatgpt-and-data-science-projects/

7 essential cyber security tips when using ChatGPT and AI tools. (2023, March 23). Wizer Training. https://www.wizer-training.com/blog/7-cyber-security-tips-using-chatgpt-ai-tools-guide

Severino, S. (2023, February 23). Streamlining your business: Automating processes with ChatGPT and AI technologies. LinkedIn. https://www.linkedin.com/pulse/streamlining-your-business-automating-processes-chatgpt-severino/

6 upskilling strategies in the world of AI. (2023). MSBC Group. https://www.msbcgroup.com/blog/Up-skilling-for-the-Future-How-to-Stay-Relevant-in-an-AI-Driven-World

Soo, J. (n.d.). Cyber and privacy risks. Marsh. https://www.marsh.com/nz/services/cyber-risk/products/cyber-privacy-risks.html#:~:text=These%20include%3A

Tanya. (2023, April 18). 10 best ChatGPT email marketing prompts. Notify Visitors. https://www.notifyvisitors.com/blog/chatgpt-email-marketing-prompts/

Thomas, M. (2019, August 27). AI and the future of jobs. Built In; Mike Thomas. https://builtin.com/artificial-intelligence/ai-replacing-jo bs-creating-jobs

Tiwari, B. (2022, August 21). Conditional statements : if, else, switch. Dot Net Tricks. https://www.dotnettricks.com/learn/c/conditional-stat ements-if-else-switch-ladder

Tran Nguyen, T. T. (2023, March 23). ChatG- PT achieves theory of mind - What does it mean? LinkedIn. https://www.linkedin.com/pulse/chatgpt-achieves-theory-mi nd-what-does-mean-thanh-tuyen-tran-nguyen/

Trends, M. (2023, March 30). How ChatGPT can help you automate and streamline your business processes. Analytics Insight. https://www.analyticsinsight.net/how-chatgpt-can-help-you-automate-a nd-streamline-your-business-processes/#:~:text=ChatGPT%20uses%20n atural%20language%20processing

Tuvar, D. (2023, February 10). 10 best ways to use ChatGPT for social media marketing. Meetanshi.com. https://meetanshi.com/blog/chatgpt -for-social-media-marketing/

UCO: ChatGPT and AI Technology. (n.d.). Univer- sity of Central Oklahoma. Retrieved May 20, 2023, from https://www.uco.edu/technology/trc/chatgpt-ai-technology#:~:te xt=It%20uses%20machine%20learning%20algorithms

V K, A. (2022, February 10). 10 industries AI will disrupt the most by 2030. Spiceworks. https://www.spiceworks.com/tech/artificial-intell igence/articles/industries-ai-will-disrupt/

Verma, E. (2018, January 24). Top 5 jobs in AI and key skills needed to help you land one. Simplilearn.com. https://www.simplilearn.com/top-a rtificial-intelligence-career-choices-and-ai-key-skills-article

Victor, A. (2023, February 27). Top 17 industry applications of Chat-GPT. Insights.daffodilsw.com. https://insights.daffodilsw.com/blog/top -17-industry-applications-of-chatgpt

Voltl, C. (2022, December 27). Revolutionize your design process with ChatGPT: 5 ways AI can boost Your creativity. Medium. https://bootcamp.uxdesign.cc/revolutionize-your-design-process-w ith-chat-gpt-5-ways-ai-can-boost-your-creativity-and-d079929676d0

What Is an API Key? - API Key Definition. (n.d.). Fortinet. https://w ww.fortinet.com/resources/cyberglossary/api-key

What is an API? - API Beginner's Guide. (n.d.). Amazon Web Services, Inc. https://aws.amazon.com/what-is/api/#:~:text=APIs%20are% 20mechanisms%20that%20enable

What is natural language processing? (n.d.) . IBM. https://www.ibm.com/topics/natural-language-processing#:~:te xt=Natural%20language%20processing%20(NLP)%20refers

Will ChatGPT transform healthcare? (2023). Nature Medicine, 29(3), 505–506. https://doi.org/10.1038/s41591-023-02289-5

Zhou, Y. (2023, March 6). 11 stunning ChatGPT powered tools that can make your life easier. TechToFreedom. https://medium.com/techtofreedom/11-stunning-chatgpt-power ed-tools-that-can-make-your-life-easier-3bb0c4e6a796

Made in the USA
Middletown, DE
30 August 2024

59955609R00080